Even Dogs Go
Home to Die

Even Dogs Go Home to Die

A Memoir

LINDA ST. JOHN

HarperCollins*Publishers*

HarperCollins books may be purchased for educational, business, or sales promotional use. For information, please write: Special Markets Department, HarperCollins Publishers Inc., 10 East 53rd Street, New York, NY 10022.

FIRST EDITION

Designed by Nicola Ferguson

Printed on acid-free paper

Library of Congress Cataloging-in-Publication Data
St. John, Linda
Even dogs go home to die / Linda St. John.—1st ed.
p. cm.
ISBN 0-06-018631-3
1. St. John, Linda   2. Adult children of alcoholics—
United States—Biography.   3. Adult children of dysfunctional families—
United States—Biography.   I. Title.
HV5132 .S7   2001
362.292'3'092—dc21
[B]   2001016605

01 02 03 04 05 WB/RRD 10 9 8 7 6 5 4 3 2 1

Jacket Illustrations by Linda St. John

Front cover: **We Didn't Fall for That Crap** (page 170)

Front flap: **"They Have Manners Over There"** (page 125)

Back flap: **"Wait in the Car"** (page 36)

Back cover: **"Ain't Dat Awful!"** (page 68)

for

Ralphie, Alice, Ann,
and my daughter, Suzi

Even Dogs Go
Home to Die

Lord Have Mercy

I don't want nobody cuttin' on my head," he kept sayin'. He went on like that for several days. Finally we convinced him he had to have the surgery. It was his only chance. They scheduled the operation for that night. We were sittin' around tellin' him not to worry. Tellin' him that everything would be ok. He was so scared. I felt like we were in a room with a man on death row. Finally some orderlies pushed a contraption in and lifted him onto it. I hugged him before they wheeled him out and he looked in my eyes. "Pray for me . . . try it," he whispered. Then he disappeared out the door . . . down the hall . . . and around the corner. I was surprised by what dad had asked me to do. I knew he had never had any use for preachers, sermons, church or heaven and hell. I sat down and wondered if god would or even could help people like us.

"I Was About Half Tight"

That's what he always used to say, but we never knew for sure how dad was gonna get in . . . whether he'd walk through the door or crawl. If he came in around midnight, when the Rat Hole closed, he'd usually be upright. But if 12 o'clock came and went with no sign of dad, we knew he'd headed out to the Midland Inn. We'd stay awake as long as we could . . . worryin'. And then we'd doze off.

So many times though we'd wake up and hear mom yellin' and screamin' real late. Once I got up and went in there. The front door was open and I could see dad was on the ground near the curb. Some men had brought him home and just pushed him outta the car. They drove off laughin'. Mom went out and tried to help him. He had to come up the stairs on his hands and knees. He stumbled around inside, grabbed the curtains to steady himself and jerked em right off the wall.

He threw up everywhere and then he tried to get in the closet to take a piss. Mom grabbed him and cried, "Dat's not dee batroom, St. John." He turned around and growled "Oooh . . . you moved it again?" I put the pillow over my head. The next morning I got up for school and just dressed and left. The place smelled so bad. Mom's cheap curtains layin' in puke.

2

"Why Can't You Kids Talk Right?"

We all had to take speech therapy . . . just a step above special ed. They didn't know what to make of us. We were white trash hicks with a real weird accent. We weren't retarded or stupid or slow in the head but we had so much trouble with the English language. Mom corrupted us so much. And the made up words we used because of her: gurkin und schmorn und bunzel und durst und schpinnie am morgen bringt kummer und sorgen. We just didn't fit in in southern Illinois with our crazy lingo. I guess people around there hadn't gotten over who ever it was they'd lost in WWII. I remember the teacher would holler, "Just say this, that and them . . . can't you say these words at all?" I would look at her and try so hard but all I could come up with was dees, dat und dem. She'd just stare at me. She never smiled. She knew I was some kind of over seas half mongrel.

War Casualty

Dad beat the hell outta Junior Gurley one day. Kicked his ass all around the yard. And Junior was a big man, maybe 6 feet tall. Dad was only 5 feet 8, but he was stout and broad and mean. Everybody was drinkin', my aunts and uncles and older cousins. They had a big old tub of long necks on ice. Somehow, the conversation turned to the war and how awful those Germans were. That's when Junior looked dad right in the eye and said with disgust, "And to think that you went over there and married you a no account kraut." Dad was on that stupid bastard so fast. He didn't even say a word. Just knocked him down and punched him 50 times in the face. Grampa got around behind dad and tried to restrain him. When he lifted dad, Junior rolled over and started crawlin'. Dad got loose from grampa and picked Junior up and threw him out in the road. He lay there in the gravel, moanin'. One of his shoes had come off. Dad picked it up and threw it at him. "She ain't a German, you son of a bitch," he yelled. "She's a Hungarian . . . and don't you fergit it."

Final Payment

Somehow, dad knew he was in real trouble so he wanted to pay off the house for mom. I came home and took them up to the City Savings and Loan. He was wearing a short sleeve summer shirt with a plastic pocket saver full of mostly nothin'. He had on dirty pants and ink splattered shoes. He'd come directly from the factory. Mom dressed for the occasion. Put on red polyester flairs and a low-cut, yellow, knit, scoop-neck, tit bitch top. We marched into the bank and he proceeded to write that final check and get his little payment book updated and stamped. He proudly asked for the deed to "our place" and was informed by the rude and impatient teller that it would arrive by mail and that stupid bastard just looked at us like it was no big deal for trash like us to be "home owners" and somehow, god damn it to hell, no balloons went up or fire crackers banged, no banner unfurled to celebrate this great achievement (which we knew was a great achievement indeed . . . making that last payment) and dad just said "ok" and put the little book away and the pen back in the pocket saver and we turned to leave. But of course, mom unable to suffer her hurt in silence turns to the teller and says, "Vel, you coult haf at least given us a pencil . . . or a key chain."

"He Can't Fill Out Anyting?"

After I left, mom kept callin' and sayin', "Someting ees wrong vid yer vater Landa . . . someting ees wrong vid yer vater." "What do you mean," I asked her. "Vel," she said, "He ees having a lot of trooble vid dee puzzles." "Mom, is he doin' his puzzles?" "No Landa no. Dats vat I mean. He spreads dem all over dee table und jist looks at dem." I called my sister.

"It's Grade 4"

Finally, Alice was able to make dad go . . . I mean what choice did he have at that point? He couldn't even hardly talk anymore . . . somethin' was eatin' up his words. He knew it and when the pain got to where it felt like someone was hittin' him in the head with a sledge hammer, he got in the car. The technician at Passavant sent him on to Springfield with an X ray that didn't look good. They put him in a room on the 6th floor with a little old lady who was strapped to her bed. She just stared at the ceiling and kept cryin' out, over and over again, "Are you gonna whup me, honey . . . Are you gonna beat me . . . Are you gonna whup me honey . . . Are you gonna beat me?" Dad would jerk his head in her direction. He tried to get outta bed. He was confused and upset . . . concerned for that old woman. He wanted to do something for her. Finally we had to go and I thought about dad alone in that hospital room with that crazy sick old lady hollerin' about beatin's and whuppin's. I know it must of been hell for him to spend the night there . . . I know he must of thought about what he'd done to mom. I saw the way he reached for her hand the next day when we got there. I saw how he didn't want to let it go.

Irish Jig

Sometimes when dad would come home drunk and hungry, he'd take a notion . . . and tap dance a little. He'd jump all around . . . kickin' his feet . . . hoppin' up and down on the linoleum. It was funny. We loved it when dad danced. It usually meant he'd won a little something at poker. Mom always tried to get him to stop. "You are goink to tear des haus down, St. John." He didn't pay her any attention. He'd glide and spin and click his hard shoes on the kitchen floor. And then he'd fry potatoes. He kept his feet movin' in front of the stove as he stirred those spuds. He'd have a fork in one hand and a beer in the other. We ate ours with salt and pepper and home made ketchup. And then dad would finish his plate and talk about that "one-eyed" potato, "that could've made us a million dollars." We had grown it ourselves, by accident . . . it was a "mutant" and unlike most potatoes that grow lots of sprouts and rot, this was a "keeper." Real good for grocers on the shelf and house wives under the sink. Dad put afew aside for seed potatoes. They were on the back porch and one night they froze . . . there went our fortune. We never again found the one-eyed potato after that, and we dug alot of rows lookin'. Dad still hoped to find one though. He wouldn't even peel a store bought tater unless he'd examined it carefully. Sometimes he'd be lookin' at one and then he'd holler. "This is it . . . I've got one . . . I've finally got one." And when we tried to look at it, he'd just laugh and hold it high above his head as he hopped around . . . his feet clobberin' the floor.

All It Needed Was
A Little Freon

Once dad came into some money and we got us a great big old used upright deep freezer. We put it in Ralphie's "room" just off the kitchen. And we started fillin' it up. We didn't can so many vegetables that year 'cause dad said they'd come outta the freezer so fresh we'd think it was June in January. We were so inspired by the freezer. Dad even got little special bags and boxes 'cause he'd heard about freezer burn and didn't want to risk it.

It was fun bringin' in vegetables from our garden at gramma's and packaging everything up properly. Dad would start the ball rollin' and then head out for a beer. We loved snappin' the green beans, huskin' the corn, slicin' the carrots. Dad even brought home extra meat when he could. A pork shoulder, then a chuck roast, hamburger that we shaped into patties, chicken legs and sausage. And we even bagged up all the surplus bass and blue gill that we caught. I would be at school thinkin' . . . we got it made . . . we have food at home and our supper will taste so good.

But that stupid freezer didn't even run 6 months. I came in one afternoon and mom was in tears. She was moppin' and cussin'. All our food was on the table, spoiled and stinkin' . . .

water runnin' everywhere. The only stuff we could eat was the peaches and strawberries. Everything else we had to throw out. Couldn't even give the meat to the dog . . . it was so green and rotten. Dad just said, "I'll be god damned." He stood there with a cigarette lookin' at the mess . . . shakin' his head. That freezer sat there unplugged for years. We went back to cannin' . . . it was safer in the long run.

Animal Rights

When I was a kid me and dad went huntin' alot . . . so many hot summer days way out in the woods. There was alot of sittin', lookin' and listenin'. "Over there," dad would whisper pointin' to the top of a hickory tree. He'd raise his shot gun and blast away. It was a shower of branches and leaves and twigs and nuts. And then finally our supper hit the ground . . . a red squirrel. We'd try to come home with as many as we could get. Fried up in a skillet . . . they were good eatin' . . . with biscuits and gravy. Sometimes it was all we had. We cleaned em on a big rock in the back yard. Dad would sharpen his pocket knife and cut their heads off and take the guts out. He'd peel their skin, fur and all, right off their bodies, and cut their little feet off. We always saved the tails. Nobody got queasy or puked and threw up. We didn't know it was a murderous ordeal. We didn't know about animal rights. We would have NEVER got that anyway . . . ANIMAL RIGHTS.

We Watched
and Waited

We all hoped that the big dark area in the X ray was just an infection. Maybe an abcessed tooth had drained up into his head. Maybe it was some kind of poisoning from the booze. Maybe it was a cyst. Maybe that's just the way our dad's brain looked.

Dad Didn't Need
No Savin'

Once Rev. Rist came by to shame us into goin' to church. It was an evening in spring. Mom let him in and then went to make him a cup of coffee. Dad didn't even get up from the couch. He hardly acknowledged the guy. He just went right on readin' the paper and smokin'. Mr. Rist sat down and said something about how he'd sure enough enjoy seein' us in church come Easter. Dad ignored him. But I could tell dad was gettin' agitated. He was startin' to cough and grunt. Mom came back and sat the Reverend's instant coffee down. She looked over at dad. Then the preacher said some more stuff about Sunday Services and how nice it is for families to worship together. And how it's important if we want to be saved and our souls go to heaven. And then Mr. Rist said directly to dad, "Mr. St. John, you want to go to heaven don't you? You want to be saved and not burn in hell for eternity." Dad narrowed his eyes at the good Rev. and then growled real mean, "Don't try to put ME on the spot with this bullshit." He threw the paper down and walked out.

"You Ain't Gettin' Nothin'"

We couldn't believe that other kids got money on a weekly basis for doin' chores. This was astounding to us because we helped out and never thought of askin' for a penny. I mowed the lawn, shoveled snow and raked leaves. I hauled clinkers and coal and pulled weeds. Dad just said kids were expected to work. He said nobody got a free ride in this life time. He talked about all he had to do when he was a boy. He said he was diggin' wells by hand when he was 12 years old. He said he was hitch hikin' down to the orchards to pick fruit. He said he was in the fields with a hoe come sun up. And all this on top of what he had to do at home. I listened to everything he said but I wanted an allowance so bad I asked for one anyway. I said, "I want a dollar a week." He just stared at me . . . then he laughed so loud. He really got a big kick outta that request.

Honesty . . . as a Policy

Once when I was 8 years old, I was home, hopin' the first of the month would roll around so dad could afford to get me some shoes. By the third day, I was tired of waitin'. I scrounged in the basement and found a pair left behind by the people who'd rented the shack before us and off I marched. The minute I hit the play ground, I was surrounded by kids starin' at me. One ugly little girl stepped forward and barked, "Where ya been at lately, Linda?" "Sick," I lied. Then she announced, "Well, Alice said you couldn't come 'cause you didn't have any shoes." "I do too," I quickly replied . . . "jist look." And I pointed to my feet and the filthy, mismatched, mildewed, black and white saddle shoes laced up with string. They all looked down and laughed. I went the rest of the day with my feet pulled up under my chair and after school I ran home cryin', charged in the house and slapped Alice till she cried . . . "Why did you tell those kids?" I screamed, "Why did you tell those stupid kids?" "They asked me where you were at Linda," she sobbed . . . "they asked me where you were at."

"Could I Stay
for Supper?"

When I was little I didn't have many friends. At least not for long. I usually wore out my welcome so fast. I'd go over to their houses and eat all I could get my hands on. For a while I was workin' the Debbie Foote connection. Her dad was a Baptist minister. I really liked Debbie and not just for the cookies and milk her mom had waitin' after school. I was over there one time and I ate nearly a whole pan of chocolate chip bars. I knew they had been reserved for some church function. Her mom was so mad; she threw me out. That next week I found out that Debbie's brother had committed a terrible awful sin . . . he'd gotten his girlfriend pregnant. She said the whole house hold was goin' nuts. They were all cryin' and crazy. Rev. and Mrs. Foote just up in arms . . . how could this happen . . . where did they go wrong . . . had the good lord deserted them . . . what were they gonna do now? Debbie told me everything. I went home with her that afternoon. They didn't even notice me when I walked in the house. I didn't figure they would. I knew they'd have alot more on their minds than a hungry 5th grader.

Diagnosis

Pearson was a brusk and cold s.o.b. He kept asking dad all kinds of things. Holding up a fork "What's this?" "Who's the president?" "What year is it?" Dad just said "Go to hell" to almost all the questions. He wanted outta there. He was mad. "Ain't nothin' wrong with me that a Falstaff won't fix." Pearson thumped on the X ray that he was holding and decreed, "You'll need more than a beer to cure this." He marched out of the room. We followed him into the hall. "The configurations of the blood vessels indicate it's malignant and aggressive," he said. My knees started to give way. I had to lean up against the wall. "This tumor is as big as a hen's egg," he said and then the bastard just turned and walked off.

"Just My Luck"

The next day we were all in the room and Pearson came in with his charts and records and results. He just looked at our dad and said, "You have a very large grade 4 sarcoma of the brain. It is a malignant primary tumor. We need to operate immediately and follow up with radiation therapy." Dad just shook his head . . . grunted and then groaned . . . "damn . . . damn." Pearson left the room. We stood there lookin' at dad. Then mom jumped up and pranced over to his bed. She grabbed his hand and cheerfully announced, "Don't vorry . . . vee are going to beat dis ting babe . . . vee are going to beat dis ting."

Fine Fare

In a big way, mom saw his illness as affording her an opportunity to "eat out." Even if it was just the hospital cafeteria in the basement. She began chattering early in the morning about what she was gonna get that afternoon when we went to visit dad (who had never taken her anywhere). Her focus was the toasted cheese or the chicken sticks and of course what kind of dessert might be on the menu. "Vel, ets Friday und dey may haf dee lemon pie Landa," she'd announce as we drove up to see him. He was layin' there with a tube up his dick and a huge tumor in his brain. We wouldn't be in the room for 30 minutes and she'd be wantin' to "go down stairs." Dad would start hollerin' to make sure she didn't run off with his smokes. She'd take a 2nd pack of Winstons out of her purse and lay that spare on his night stand, and out she'd go, usually with Alice who would bark at her "You better have your own damn money." I would wheel dad down to the visitors lounge where he would light one cigarette after another until they returned. Finally mom would hop around the corner, sit down on the vinyl couch and proceed to tell us just how good the fishwich was.

Meat, Milk,
Vegetables and Cereal

We had NEVER been a coupon clippin' outfit. Dad wasn't interested. He wasn't about to take a chance on the discount card, the rebate slip or the 10 cents off flyer on whatever he was buyin'. He just paid full price without the benefit of any of those money savin' schemes. He was afraid some one in the check out line might think he was usin' food stamps or worse yet . . . welfare vouchers. So when he was grocery shoppin' he wasn't gonna stand there with anything except CASH in hand.

Dad wasn't gonna let anyone do anything for him . . . he wasn't no dead beat on the dole . . . "I can take care of mine," he'd say. But we were hungry alot when we were kids. We'd go to bed and dream of food . . . we'd drift off planning elaborate "gourmet" meals. We didn't talk that much about toys or games or clothes. We'd lay there and make grocery lists. Canned ravioli, pork-n-beans, macaroni and cheese, fried chicken, sliced tomatoes, hot dogs on hot dog buns (not bread), Hostess cupcakes, canned peaches and then chocolate covered cherries.

Once I showed dad the poster I'd made in 6th grade. "These are the 4 Food Groups," I said, "We *need* the 4 Food

Groups." He actually looked at the chart and sort of grunted and then he laughed out loud. He said too bad he hadn't known about all them fine possibilities when he was a boy . . . maybe he wouldn't of had to eat so many blackbirds, crawdads and possums.

She Gave Him Some
of the Cookies
to Take Home

I believe the Parks family was the only bunch around worse off than us. There must have been at least 8 kids. The dad was a no account and the mom was sick with a liver disease that turned her skin a weird awful color. She'd stand on the porch . . . a baby-shit yellow stick figure with dark raccoon eyes. She'd stand there and watch us . . . just lost in her big flowered house dresses. She couldn't even care for her children at that point.

I remember one time we were all out playin' across town in some rich neighborhood and a Parks boy went right up and knocked on the back door of a big fine house. He asked somebody's mom for somethin' to eat. He just said, "I'm hungry . . . I'll eat anything . . . even if it's rotten." The lady just sort of stood there and looked at him. She patted him on the head and then brought out some cookies. It was a miracle. She carried a silver tray down the steps. We crowded around. They were so good . . . home made . . . somethin' we never got.

Later I thought about that boy beggin' for food . . . or garbage. We had us some lean times in our family too but we refused to eat anything spoiled. Somehow though we didn't ever really feel that we were that much better off than those Parks kids and we didn't feel that sorry for em. Maybe we should have but we just figured that as far as we were concerned, drawin' the line at rotten food when you're hungry isn't really that much better than goin' ahead and eatin' it.

Jane Was Lucky

I went over to Jane's house alot. Her mother never threw me out. Mrs. Huffman didn't care how much I ate. She always had Cokes in the ice box and some kind of good treats. She always asked me if I'd had enough. One winter Jane had an ice skating party. They owned a bunch of land that had a pond on it. Some parents volunteered to drive all the kids out there. I rode with Jane and her mom. It wasn't too far. Everybody started pullin' up and gettin' outta their cars. They all ran down to the pond and put on their ice skates. One of the dads made a big fire. I stayed up there and hung around with all the the grown ups. Mrs. Huffman put milk and sugar and cocoa in a big pot and started heatin' it up. I looked down there at the popular rich kids laughin' and havin' fun. Somebody's mom said, "Why don't you go ice skate?" I said, "I forgot my skates." They looked back and forth at each other. Then Mrs. Huffman laughed and said, "Oh isn't that the way it always works . . . I almost forgot mine too."

Doctor's Orders

Because of what ever medicine he was on for the cancer, they didn't want him drinkin'. They said alcohol was a no no. And we were just astounded at how quickly he was able to give that up. We couldn't believe it . . . after all he'd put us through. In a way it was almost disappointing to see the booze fall away from dad so easily. He didn't get the D.T.'s. He didn't even get the shakes. He just quit over night. But we sure enough remembered when he was a big time drinkin' man.

They Come by
That Meanness
Honestly

I guess dad's drinkin' problem stems mostly from him bein' Irish and Indian. I can't remember a time when dad didn't drink. But we never thought he was an alcoholic. Hell, he got up and went to work. That's how you measured a drunk back then. If a guy could get up and clock in . . . he wasn't no bum. But so much of dad's meager check went for booze. We suffered alot especially at the end of the month when he had to decide between food and his 6 packs. Somehow, there was always money for beer. It was a daily thing . . . dad goin' out. Grampa was a big drinker too. Whiskey was his choice. Him and his brothers and cousins would head out to the Shawnee National Forest. They'd be out there camped for weeks. They'd hunt alittle but mostly they'd play poker, drink and fight. Once grampa and Willard went round and round. They were wrasslin', fallin' down in the creek, mad and drunk and crazy, and first thing you know . . . there's a knife and grampa's ear is nearly sliced off. But his dad was a country doctor . . . just sewed it back on. When we combed grampa's hair . . . we saw the scars. He'd gotten his scalp cut so bad once . . . the whole top of his head just flapped up like the open lid on a tin can of beans. You could see the stitches all the way around his forehead. We liked grampa's face . . . scars and all. He looked so much like an Indian . . . his tomahawk nose . . . his thick hair . . . his dark eyes. His mom was a full blooded real Indian. They argue over what kind but probably Cherokee. Although my aunt Maudie always hoops and hollers and then throws her head back and yells, "Apache . . . god damn it . . . blood thirsty Apache."

"Where's My Gun?"

He come in late one night . . . hollerin' for his gun. I woke up from the racket he was makin' scroungin' in the closet—stompin' around, kickin' things over. "I'm gonna kill em," he yelled. "I'm gonna kill em." I woke up my sisters and me and Alice and Ann sneaked out the back door and hid behind the forsythia bush in the back yard. I could hear him hoorawin' through the kitchen window. "Where's my .38 . . . where's my .38?" We stood quietly in the cool spring air watching stars shoot across the dark heavens—hoping it wasn't us he wanted to kill but rather some so and so down at the tavern.

Alice's Sarcoma

When we got the for sure diagnosis on dad, Alice wanted to run right out and have a CAT scan of *her* brain. She was worried she might have a tumor too. But Pearson said he'd been in business 25 years and this thing didn't "run in families." She got all crazy anyway. Maybe somehow she knew what was going to happen to her. Maybe that's why she was so awful to be around. Maybe that's why she looked at mom's forehead one day and said to her, "You only have 6 weeks to live . . . that mole is gonna take over your face." I hated my sister for that. She always poured over medical journals and disease periodicals. A fat house wife obsessed with obscure sickness—leprosy, elephantiasis, parasites and worms, spirochetes and carbuncles, creatures resulting from Thalidomide. She is the classic hypochondriac who will frantically clutch her chest and holler heart failure after eating four chili dogs with everything. But when that patch of skin wouldn't go away, when she kept complaining of it, and finally went in to have it checked, I was just horrified at how much of Alice's nose that friggin' quack actually took off.

"It Helps to Talk"

When we'd visit dad at the hospital, Alice would park herself on a chair at the end of the hall, where visitors would sit to have a smoke or just some time away from the room of a loved one in the intensive care ward. These people were sad and bewildered. They were waitin' and hopin'—often silent, staring off, caught up in their own anguish. Sometimes babbling, revealing the most personal things to the total stranger sitting next to them. "There's no hope," I heard her say loudly, as I pushed dad down the hall toward the lounge. "The doctor says its the worst kind of cancer there is. He doesn't have long." Dad jerked when he heard that. He twisted around to look at me. His dark eyes did not leave my face. "Why, that's not us . . . is it?" he asked slowly. "No dad," I said as I turned the chair around and quickly wheeled it the other way. "That's not us."

They Cut Out
What They Could

It didn't take all that long. Just afew hours and then they wheeled dad out of the operating room. He was actually awake. HE WAS ALIVE! He was smiling. He wanted a cigarette. The nurses and doctors and attendants couldn't believe how strong he was. They told us everything went fine. They said he could have him a smoke but not until they got him off the oxygen. "You don't want to blow this place from here to kingdom come, do you?" they joked. Dad laughed. We laughed too. We were so happy to laugh. They pushed him on to the recovery room. It was real late so we just sat in the lounge and waited. We drank coffee and listened to Alice go on and on about her health worries. Finally the sun came up.

He Wasn't About to
Quit the Cigs

We went up to see dad. Pearson was in the room. He said dad could go home in afew days. He said in a week they'd start the radiation treatment. He wrote out a prescription for some pills and that was that. We stayed awhile. Dad was sittin' up in bed smokin' like a fiend. I didn't see him strike a single match. He'd just take each burned down butt and light the next cig. A nurse come in. She looked around the room and then went over and raised a window. She said, "Phew, we sure don't want that smoke alarm goin' off do we?" She laughed. We didn't think it was that funny. We were just too tired and wore out to joke any more about dad's smokin'. It was awful to watch him crumple that many empty packs in one afternoon.

Sorry for Somethin'

At 1st when dad got sick we hoped he might think about things . . . maybe say he was sorry for all the bullshit and meanness. That would have made a world of difference to us.

But we waited and waited and nothin' happened . . . nothin' changed. He just kept sayin' what he always used to say when he got too drunk . . . that he "didn't mean to hit *me* in the face with a knuckle ball." Hell, I didn't care about that pitch. So what?

I could catch a fast ball, a curve ball and even a slider. Who gives a shit if that knuckle ball hopped up over my out stretched glove? I wasn't mad at dad. But he never forgot it . . . ever.

He was layin' there in his hospital bed lookin' at me . . . still mumblin' about that time he hit me in the nose. Alice said he brought it up all the time. Comin' home from his radiation treatments she said he went on and on about all that blood on my shirt . . . how I'd run in the house cryin' . . . how he "wished to hell he wouldn't have thrown that pitch." And at Thanksgiving we were all together, sittin' around the table, Ralphie, Alice and Ann lookin' at him . . . waitin' to be noticed . . . waitin' and hopin' for afew words that would never come their way. I sat there too . . . but I knew there wasn't gonna be any major miracles. Dad was immune to the revelations inspired by cancer. He never thought about how he had treated us. We just looked at him. We had to settle for listening to his insane regret about a pitch he threw 30 years ago. It was nuts. It seemed like the only thing he figured he ever really did wrong to *us* was to hit *me* in the nose with a knuckle ball . . . shit, we didn't need an apology for an accident.

"Wait in the Car"

We were mostly uncivilized . . . just wild beasts. There's no way we could have gone on a family vacation. And he did have time off in the summer. We never got to go anywhere. No Disneyland, no Six Flags over Mid-America, no Yellowstone National Park. He wouldn't have taken us even if he'd had the money. Hell, just the hour it took to get to gramma's ended up with stops along the road cause somebody had "touched" somebody in the back seat and all hell broke loose. He'd turn around and yell at us to quit fightin'. He'd start hollerin' about his ulcer. Finally, he'd have to pull over and take his belt off. He'd jerk us outta the car one by one and we'd get it good. I know it was a spectacle. People would be drivin' by . . . lookin' . . . pointin'. I always prayed it was nobody we knew. We'd pile back in cryin' . . . all snot and tears. He'd growl "AT EASE" real mean. He'd light a cig and take off. We'd sit there silently starin' out the window, wipin' our faces . . . feelin' like shit . . . wonderin' why we couldn't be good . . . why we just couldn't be good.

Season's Greetings

We're out scrounging Coke bottles to cash in for a 2 dollar tree from the gas station. It's Christmas Eve day and they still have afew left. They're all reduced to the same price now, so we drag home the biggest one and coat hanger it upright on a little lawn table in the front room. We get out all the cigarette wrappers we've been saving for weeks and use them to cover cardboard. And now, we have silver stars of all sizes. We've gathered pine cones and sweet gum balls and with the glitter and glue that I "borrowed" from school soon they're bright and shiny and spinning on our tree. Only afew bulbs come on when we plug in the lights. We throw on the tinsel that we saved from last year and on the top, I place a polka dot angel I made from a Wonder Bread bag. I use some of the ribbons that were thrown out after the gift exchange between the kids. I dug them out of the wastebasket that day at school. I waited and waited and finally . . . just me and the teacher. (I took the pretty wrapping paper too.) We look at our beautiful tree and we smell the branches and then we get ready for church. We sing in the Christmas Eve service and participate in the Jesus skit. We go mostly because after the final carol is sung, we get a little brown paper sack. It's full of goodies and handed to us by the nice man at the door. We each request an extra for our brother who is "sick and couldn't come." The guy smiles and gives it to us. And out we go . . . 3 little girls trundling along through the dark cold night air. Our legs are frozen when we get home. But we get oranges . . . good oranges and it's worth it. We get salted peanuts in the shell. Chocolate drops and a candy cane. There's a Hershey bar . . . a big one. We sit on the floor by our tree and eat our church treats and then we go to bed. We get up the next morning . . . there are no real presents tied up special with ribbons waiting for us. It's just the stuff we've made for each other or found . . . a mouse pin carved from a little piece of wood, a bird nest with 2 speckled eggs, a pretty piece of purple quartz and a neat plant fossil from the strip mine. And that's what I will take for show and tell when school starts back. The other kids will have stories of bikes and dolls and coats and shoes. They will talk about coloring books and paint by number sets. Wagons and sleds. Board games and ice skates. But who cares about all that old stuff . . . NOT ME! Because this year, I will have a *fern* . . . a fern that's a hundred million years old.

Singed

One night in early spring the temperature dropped down so low that our box of baby rabbits on the back porch died. We were so upset because these had lived the longest of all the survivors we'd ever collected. Every time we burnt the fields off it was the same thing. We took sticks and tried to chase the rabbits out of hiding . . . we tried to get them to run off. Lots of em did but far too many just froze right where they were in the dry thick brush that would soon go up in flames around them. Some babies survived the scorching. They had burrowed down into the cool earth. "Here's one," Alice would exclaim. "And another . . . and another." We walk through the charred ground looking everywhere. We pick them up and put them in a card board box lined with soft rags. We take them home and feed them with an eye dropper. Dad always said a baby rabbit didn't stand a chance on cow's milk. "They need their mother." But this time our rabbits had made it a whole week. Some were even eatin' grass. So that cold night when we looked in the box and they weren't movin', we felt horrible. When dad got home we cried, "The rabbits froze . . . the rabbits froze." He was drunk already but he opened him another beer. He staggered out to the porch and then brought the box in and put it on a chair close to the stove. "They'll warm up," he said. We didn't know what to think. We just stood silently . . . staring at the rabbits and soon they actually started opening their eyes and movin' their ears and twitchin' their noses. We jumped up and down! We couldn't believe it. Dad had brought them back to life! They lived alittle longer but one by one they just quit eatin'. We knew that was it this time. "One of the hazards of the game," as dad would say. So we buried them in the back yard where we had buried box full after box full of baby rabbits before them.

Too Damn Hot
to Hooraw

I remember afew times in my life when dad would actually come home after a hard day at work with a bag of lemons. It didn't happen often . . . but once in a great while in the summer when it was real hot he'd bring us some. Come evening he'd slice em in half and squeeze the juice in a pitcher. He'd throw in some ice and a cup of sugar and he'd stir and stir till it dissolved. We stood there watchin' . . . astounded that he would do this. Then he'd pour us some in jelly jars and out the back door we'd hop . . . feelin' special . . . feelin' like we were even rich 'cause it was night time and 90 degrees and we had somethin' good to drink . . . somethin' besides water. We'd sip our refreshing beverage and listen to the crickets and frogs and feel the hot breeze on our faces. Dad wouldn't even have to yell at us or beat us. We weren't fightin' or hoorawin' or causin' trouble. We were just sittin' around in those cheap lawn chairs . . . swingin' our legs back and forth . . . drinkin' lemonade . . . laughin' and gettin' along . . . like other kids and dad was sittin' there too, in peace . . . nursin' his beer . . . fixin' to turn on the radio for the Cardinal game. It was wonderful. It was a miracle . . . those few times back then . . . when somehow . . . we were like a family and able to actually take it easy . . . just take it easy in the back yard.

Pumpkin Breakdown

We broke down late one night miles from no where. The car just got hot and finally give out . . . so there we sat along the hard road. Me scared. Dad mad . . . drunk . . . smokin' cigarettes . . . cussin' . . . hollerin'. "Shit," he said. "No wonder . . . there must be a ton of pumpkins in this car." He lit another cig. "Let's go," he growled. We got out and started walkin'. It was so late. Nobody was goin' by on old route 13. Finally we made it to the cross roads and caught a ride with a guy headed west. He dropped us off on Main Street and we got home about 2 in the morning. I tried to sleep but all I could do was worry about my cash crop stranded out there. I got up the next morning and dad was already gone. I had to go to school. When I got home that afternoon, the car was in the drive way and all my pumpkins were stacked neatly on the porch. I didn't know I had that many. I was jumpin' up and down. Dad came out and said, "Yeah . . . you better be happy 'cause by god I'm through . . . that's it. I ain't ever gonna haul so many god damn pumpkins again in that beat-up Chevrolet . . . I don't care how drunk I am."

Dad Didn't Have
Many Choices

The first time I got up and my skinny legs were criss crossed in red whelps I didn't know what had happened. I ran in the kitchen. "Lookie. . . . lookie," I cried. Mom turned around and said, "He beat you goot last night Landa . . . I hot told heem to." I just stood there lookin' at her. I tried so hard to remember the beatin' . . . but I just couldn't. I only remember goin' to bed . . . crawlin' under the cover . . . closin' my eyes.

Dad let us have it like that afew times at 3 in the morning when he'd get in real drunk and she wouldn't give him any peace cause of all the "trooble" we'd caused while she was stuck there and he was out "enjoyin' " himself. He refused to take her. He would rather pull off his belt and jerk us outta bed when we were sleepin'. He did it to shut her up . . . to just shut mom the hell up because what else could he do? By god, he wasn't gonna take her anywhere. Dad wasn't gonna let her put on a fancy dress and fix her hair and go out with HIM. I remember when he used to say to her, ". . . I ain't EVER gonna take YOU around human beings."

Pickin' Up Dad

We pulled up down below at the hospital and a nurse pushed him out the double doors toward the car. The bandage was off his head now and the stitches were out. But he still had the ink marks on his scalp—guide posts for the radiation treatment. I helped him from the wheel chair into the front seat. His head was still swollen above the ear and that huge U shaped suture made me moan out loud.

I looked at the back of his head for 55 miles. Shaved bald from the operation . . . a little bit of red hair on the right side that wasn't involved.

Pearson couldn't say what caused it . . . the farmin' chemicals around here, the fuel oil spill in the drinking water years ago, the 6 packs preempting food, the solvents at the factory, the nicotine, the meanness—maybe all of it . . . maybe none.

Dad lit another cig and then put his hand up to his head. He didn't rub it, just kind of patted it . . . like and old person's stiff hand would touch a child.

He Never Cut
Ralphie Any Slack

I wasn't surprised when afew days after dad come home from the hospital . . . Ralphie said he had to get goin'! He said he had to get back to work. It was a long drive back down to southern Illinois. He packed his little bag and shook dad's hand.

Then he told dad that he'd come up again before too long. Dad said ok. Me and Alice and Ann stayed alittle longer. We tried to cheer dad up. We talked about things that might be a pleasant memory for him.

Survival of the Fittest

Dad never had any patience for the "trouble we caused" and "trouble" could be anything like gettin' sick or gettin' hurt. We knew from the get go that we were on our own. That's why when Ralphie crashed his bike real bad once . . . he didn't want to go home.

He was scared . . . he was cryin', "Dad's gonna beat me . . . dad's gonna beat me."

A man drivin' by saw the wreck. He stopped and ran over. He looked at Ralphie layin' there. He said, "Are you hurt little boy . . . do you want me to take you home?" Ralphie said, "No . . . no . . . I don't need to go home." He struggled to his feet. "See?" he said, "I'm ok." The man wasn't convinced. I could tell by the way he stood there lookin' at us. But he got in his car and drove off. Ralphie sat back down. We waited there for awhile and finally he was able to get on his bike. We went out in the woods. We just hung around . . . killin' time . . . waitin' till we knew dad would have headed out for a drink. Ralphie was so worried about dad seein' him. He figured he might not look so bad in the morning . . . maybe no one would notice he'd been in a wreck. . . that he'd gone over the handle bars and hit a tree. Finally we rode home after dark. We went in the house and Ralphie washed up and doctored himself. He come outta the bathroom and said, "I feel alright . . . dad won't be mad . . . I won't have to go to the hospital . . . he won't be out anything." I stood there lookin' at Ralphie's face covered with cuts and bruises and glowing like a camp fire from all the Mercurochrome.

Ralphie's Braces

One day Ralphie said, "Lookie Linda." And I looked. His jaws closed tight . . . a number 2 yellow pencil between the gap of his clinched teeth. His lips pulled back. Walking around like that . . . one walrus fang showing that something wasn't right . . . his teeth to stick out like that. And when dad come home, Ralphie put the pencil in and made the announcement again . . . "I need braces." Dad stopped what he was doin', he looked at Ralphie real mean and then just growled, "Shit."

What's a Top Sheet?

We were cold alot when we lived in that little shack in Carterville. Ice was all over the windows in the winter, especially in the back room where we slept—farthest from the stove.

We doubled up and threw coats over us. Ann was in a baby bed in the next room with mom and dad. She cried alot and got mad. At age 1, she would stand up as tall as she could on the tips of her toes and scream and yell and shake her little fist at you (for no reason). Sometimes when mom would get up early, she would put Ann in bed with dad. Most of the time he'd put her back in her baby bed because she fussed and kicked so much. One morning she was really screamin' because he had just plopped her on the floor. She didn't have a diaper on. The bare linoleum was freezin' cold and Ann peed right where she sat. He just rolled over and ignored her. She was cryin' so loud. I got up and walked through there and picked her up. I took her into the stove room and I warmed her by the fire. No fist shakin' now, she just held onto me. I was 7 years old and I sat there wondering why dad would put her on the floor on such a cold morning and leave her there bare-assed cryin' in a puddle of piss.

Hummin' a Tune

When I was little, I wanted to play the saxophone or the bag pipes or the accordian. I begged dad to let me take lessons in school. "We could rent somethin' . . . it don't cost much . . . you pay by the month . . . please daddy." His answer was always the same, "I ain't got the money . . . now go on." I knew to quit askin' . . . I knew the musical instrument wasn't gonna happen. Mom did play the radio sometimes. She'd be in the kitchen in the morning listenin' to Tennessee Ernie Ford, Perry Como and Patsy Cline. That was a short lived deal. The radio blew a tube and we never got it fixed. There was some music at church. We tried to follow along with the hymns but believe me, no one wanted us in the choir. I never heard gramma sing or grampa or my aunts or uncles . . . nobody. Once in awhile dad might hum an old army song but that's about it. We just weren't a musical bunch. When I was 14, I scrounged up a used record player. It was a wooden box covered in light green sparkle cloth with a snap off detachable speaker. We put on a Beatle record and dad got so mad. He stormed in there drunk with a beer in his hand. "Shut dat crap off." He kicked the record player and the needle jumped onto the cloth. He yelled, "I ain't interested in this hip-pie shit." Then he hollered all about the pinko bastards out there who should just go on and get jobs 'cause by god this was America and those worthless long hairs should love it or leave it. He stumbled out of the room. Finally he went to bed. We put the record back on . . . real low. We tried to enjoy the songs but mostly we just sat there in the dark feelin' bad . . . feelin' like some kind of awful communists 'cause we wanted to listen to a little music.

Maybe She *Was* a Half Wit

Mom didn't do much to make our lives easier or happier. She couldn't. I don't believe she ever thought of herself as the Mother. She was like a 5th child . . . a competitor in a way. Dad wanted to see her as a wife, not some helpless, needy, crazy person. But that's the way she was. One day she said to me, "You know dat time he took you down to the hardware store Landa und bought all you kids bikes . . . vel, I vasn't mad but you know he NEVER asked me if I vonted von . . . he never bought *me* a bike."

"Our Only Alternative"

Mom didn't know anything about finance charges. In the end she paid nearly double what that stupid dining room set was worth. She said she didn't mind. She said, "Dat's dee only vay I could geet it, Landa." All her babysittin' money went toward that cheap junk. Five dollars a week. She took it down there and gave it to a lady at the counter. That woman wrote us a receipt and then mom would thank her and go on and on about how nice the set was and how much we were enjoyin' it but only for special occasions because other wise we had to use the old orange table etc. etc. I saw the way that clerk looked at us. She didn't smile or laugh or give a shit about us. On the way home mom talked about how much she liked those people. She said, "Dey hot done me a beek favor Landa vid dee table und chairs . . . maybe someday I can geet someting else from dat nice store."

"No Von Better Call
Me Again Like Dat"

Nobody ever covered yer back in that family. You never even got the benefit of the doubt . . . especially with mom. If a total stranger said somethin' about you . . . she'd take their word over yours any day. What ever happened was our fault. Once I defended myself against a boy on the playground. He was always pickin' on little kids and he was a big guy about to start high school. I was only 12 but I knocked him around good. I tore his shirt off and pushed him down. He got up and ran off. I went home and the phone was ringin'. It was that kid's mom. She was hollerin' so loud, I could hear every word she said. "You keep yer girl away from my boy or I'll call the cops . . . I'll sue you . . . That girl belongs in a reform school . . . They have places for girls like her . . . She has no right to beat my boy up and tear his clothes off . . . What's the matter with you lady? . . . You better teach yer kids some manners . . . If this ever happens again . . . etc. etc." Finally mom just hung up on her. She was so upset but she didn't ask me anything about what had happened. She just hollered, "Your een beek trouble Landa ven your vater geets home . . . eets yer fault dat voman hot called up and schreamed at me . . . I didn't do anyting wrong . . . I don't even know dat damn boy."

Special Mementos

Mom always liked scrap books and albums. So one year Ralphie bought her one from the dime store. There weren't many pictures of us to put in it but that didn't matter to mom. She would just cut out photographs from magazines. If any one came over she'd get out the album and flip it open to show them pictures of Zsa Zsa Gabor, Marilyn Monroe and Liz Taylor like they were members of our family. She also liked to clip articles outta the newspaper and paste those in the album. "See, dees von ees about dee beeg diamond dey hot found een Africa . . . Dees von ees about dat awful mud slide in Brazil . . . und look . . . See how much I got about dat murderer who keeld all dee leedle kids . . . 5 pages on dat animal."

Evidence That Dad
Liked Her

Alice tore her foot up so bad one time. She was ridin' her bike and somehow hit a bumper on a parked car. The sharp part of the metal cut through her sandal and way up between her toes. Nearly sliced her foot in two. She said she had no idea how bad she was hurt. She said she just wanted to go home and put a Band-Aid on it. A guy stopped though and saw all the blood. He took her to Holden Hospital inspite of her protests. Alice begged that guy not to tell dad and when she got over to the emergency room, she begged anybody and everybody who would listen not to tell dad. "He'll beat me . . . he'll beat me . . . if he finds out." Alice said the nice man who had brought her in couldn't believe dad would beat her for gettin' hurt. Alice said that guy actually went over to where dad worked and got him. Alice said she didn't know what he said to dad but he must have said somethin' 'cause when dad came in the hospital room he looked around at the doctors and nurses and then he looked at her and said, "Honey . . . are you alright?" Then he said, "Well it looks like I'll have to buy you an ice cream cone and take you to the show."

Alice said she was stunned. She couldn't believe it. He didn't even act mad. He waited till the doctor finished the stitches and then he helped Alice out the door. Alice expected that he'd just take her home but they went down to the Varsity Theater and she did get a double dip of orange sherbert and they did watch a movie. She said her foot didn't even bother her at all . . . she was so happy to just be somewhere with dad . . . she said she figured that wreck was worth it.

"I Need to Soak
My Dogs"

Alice wanted to do all she could for dad. So after one of his radiation treatments they stopped off at the foot doctor. That guy burnt off dad's planter's warts and showed him how to keep the calluses down so he could walk without pain. And he said them cut up pieces of carpeting dad was usin' for cushioning weren't any good. He said dad needed to get rid of that stuff and just go out and invest in a nice comfortable pair of shoes. Alice took him to Payless and he got two pairs for the price of one. They were real leather.

Boy's Sox and
Bug Lights

Dad's motto was "git it and growl."

You couldn't waste any time debatin' a color, a style or a size. You were supposed to just go in and grab something. Who had the luxury to "mess around" with choices. It was so nerve wracking . . . usually I walked out without anything because I couldn't take the pressure. I didn't have the confidence that dad did. He could make anything work. Once he needed sox . . . no time to read the size chart . . . so he ended up with something for a 10 year old boy. And by god he wore em. And then once we needed light bulbs. He bought 8 packs of something to use out doors to repel insects. Eventually though the whole *inside* of our house had a soft dull amber glow . . . it was like the twilight zone for months . . . people movin' in and outta shadows in every room. Finally he put a bright 100 watt bulb in the kitchen and that's what really sent the roaches running. I threw away the last burnt out little yellow bulb and we started stompin'. We must of killed a million bugs. Dad's striped kid's sox barely showin' above the top of his clompin' shoes.

Happy Easter

Once dad won money in a card game and give mom some to buy us Easter outfits. We went down to the Illinois Brokerage . . . cheapest store in town. I made mom spend most of the money on me. My dress was a pretty purple gingham with lace and ric-rac. Not much left for hats . . . we each got decorated head bands. Alice wore my old green dress with the lady bugs all over it and Ann had a little sailor dress that a neighbor give us. That was it. We went to Sunday school. It was tough to face those other kids. Those girls had nice linen spring coats, black patent leather shoes, white lace anklets, little straw pocket books and beautiful bonnets covered in ribbons and flowers. But we really wanted the chocolate bunny and the Easter egg with the gold cross that they were handin' out.

So we showed up. We sat there in our scroungy day sweaters and worn school shoes. We sat there and listened to the preacher's wife. She went on and on about the good lord and suffering. We bowed our heads and tried to think of god's only begotten son and what he'd done for *us*. We said the prayers and followed along with the songs. We did what we were supposed to do and we didn't care that everyone knew why we were really there.

What Came Around . . .
Didn't Go Around

Mom was never big on doin' anything for anybody but she sure liked to have other people do for her. It was embarrassing. She was shameless the way she'd go to the neighbors and ask for things . . . a cup of this . . . a cup of that that . . . a ride somewhere and she never offered any money for gas. And during the holidays she sure enough wasn't about giving . . . she was about receiving. She never made any kind of special delecacies to give to other people. She'd just wait for some nice somebody to feel sorry for *us* and come over with a fruit cake or a cheese plate or a box full of used clothes. She'd say, "Vel at least 'Meesus' so und so ees a goot person . . . she hat geeven us something des year." And it was amazing how she waited around expecting Christmas cards but never sent any. She wouldn't even acknowledge a generous relative who'd slip a little money in the envelope. Hell, she'd just act like she had it comin'.

Once she got so mad though . . . just bitchin' and complainin' 'cause a letter came askin' for somethin' from us. One of dad's 2nd cousins, a poor old spinster lady livin' in a shack down home wrote in mid December beggin' for money. Mom was outraged. She threw the letter down. She screamed and yelled and carried on. She said "Dat betch . . . she hot alot of nerve . . . she ees trying to geet money Landa . . . money for coal because eets so cold outside." I was shocked. Why would mom be that upset just because an old woman wanted to stay warm?

Ash Tray

Finally he come in and before he could even sit down at the kitchen table and open him a beer, she started in on him with how he should go on and beat the hell out of us . . . 'cause we'd been bad, raisin' cane, fightin', and be sure and belt us all good. "Get dis one St. John" "beat dis one" "belt all des brats" brats . . . des brats . . . brats that she was stuck with every night he went out to come back smellin', weavin', wobblin', carryin' a brown paper sack and drop himself onto a chrome and vinyl chair and slur his words but finally growl . . . clear enough for her to understand . . . "stick out yer tongue you bitch I want to put out my cigarette."

Big Plans

He rallied pretty good after the operation. Some of his words were mixed up or gone but he could still walk and even ride his bike. He went out one day and started scraping paint off the side of the garage. "Gonna get this done," he proclaimed. He had on a beige sock hat, his ink stained factory clothes and the glasses that he had repaired himself by gluing a huge nut and bolt right in the front part that rested above his nose. Something Frankenstein would wear. He was coming up with all kinds of plans to work around the place—fix it up. Finally get that roof patched, finally stop all them leaks, redo the ceiling, take up that filthy carpet, haul off that mountain of beer cans, pull all that crap out of the basement, fix the toilet, and maybe get that furnace looked at—winter was coming. He had never lifted a finger around this dump before and now, here he was after his brain surgery, a handy man, with green paint chips all over his face. I just looked at the big bolt between his eyes, and said "yeah . . . ok . . . dad."

A "Meat and Potatoes" Man

We never had any kind of "foreign foods" like lasagna or veal parmesan when we were little. Hell, we couldn't even have pizza. Dad had no interest in acknowledging the Italians by gettin' involved in their cuisine. He hated the WOPS. He cursed em and said he wished to hell he would have been old enough in the 1930s to kick the shit out of them no good bums. He said they came down from Chicago and crossed the picket lines. He said, "A lot of good men lost their minin' jobs 'cause of them scabs." So dad refused to buy "Italian bread," "Italian cheese" and "Italian sausage." And if he was ever cookin' somethin' that required oregano or garlic or olive oil, he'd just refuse to add that ingredient. "We ain't usin' 'at shit," he'd say. He'd stand there and stir a pot of soup and growl, "By god, I don't need to turn this into some kind of Dago crap."

Cook Stove

We would help grampa split kindlin', and we would gather sticks to start the fire up in the cook stove. Sometimes gramma would run a chicken down in the yard. She'd chop its head off and fry it up. And she'd cook taters and roastin' ears and make gravy. Her biscuits were so good. She'd put some flour in a bowl . . . add salt and bakin' powder and holler out a hole in the middle. That's where she'd pour in the milk and with a spoon slowly work in the sides to make a drop batter. Her recipes were in her head and by god they stayed there. Once I asked her, "Gramma, how much of this, how much of that?" She stopped mixing just long enough to turn to me and growl, "Why you put in 'till you've got enough!"

Gramma

I don't know if I ever saw gramma smile. She didn't have anything nice or pretty around the house. The linoleum was so wore off it looked like tar paper on the floor. She had two dirty rag rugs on top of black grit. On the windows, she had shear lace curtains—they were plastic. Her quilts were all heavy and dark—made from cut up old men's trousers and coats. No light floral cottons in a pretty pattern—just somber patch work squares of dull wool. The walls were blotched with coal soot belching from the stove and rain water leaking through the roof. Gramma spit in a Maxwell House coffee can—tobacco and snuff. She'd sit on the couch and peel taters in a pan resting on her lap. Wouldn't even want to cut the lights on come evening. "Cain't waste the juice" . . . just sittin' peelin' in the twilight. She had a few doilies here and there . . . nothin' to sit on them—no house plants . . . no artificial arrangements. She never had flowers in the yard . . . "don't need em" and if a stray kitten came onto the place and took to hangin' around, she wouldn't even give it a name—just cat.

"Ain't Dat Awful!"

Grampa didn't even marry gramma till he was 43 years old. She was an old maid of 29 . . . but the only possibility in town. Grampa's mother, the old squaw, had just died and he needed someone to take care of him. So gramma moved in. She loved *him,* gave him 5 kids that lived and put up with his dandy stupid ways. That was the English kickin' in. He always wore a tie. He refused to wear overalls. He had a winter hat and a summer straw. He had brown hi-tops and black ones too. He did do some gardening. He did do alittle coal minin'. But really he didn't work much at all. Just let the house come down around them. Upstairs where dad slept as a boy, you could see day light through the roof in certain places. There were buckets up there to catch the rain. And the snow that blowed in, just swirled everywhere. Lots of times in the winter dad would wake up to a light dusting on his quilt. He spent alot of time out in the woods with his dog. Huntin', fishin', tryin' to make ends meet. Puttin' somethin' on the table for him and his 4 sisters.

Dad didn't usually talk about his childhood much but sometimes when he was real drunk he'd complain alittle. It was always the same thing. He'd call grampa a dead beat . . . a no account waitin' on the relief truck. He'd take another gulp of beer . . . look us in the eye and then call grampa the worst thing he could think of: "A *Democrat* . . . a god damn somethin' fer nothin' Democrat." After that pronouncement dad would get up and stagger off to bed mumblin', "That's the way it goes . . . that's the way it goes."

Native American Remedy

Grampa was the first one to notice that big scab on my knee. I'd had it for over a year. I fell off my bike in an alley. All summer it never got better. By fall, I was pretty worried. I'd read the "warning signs" . . . a sore that won't heal. So I didn't tell anybody. I knew how much trouble I'd be in if dad found out. I could only imagine how much an amputation cost. So, as long as it didn't hurt . . . I kept my mouth shut. That next summer we were workin' in the garden. Grampa looked down and said, "What's the matter with yer leg?" "Cancer . . . I believe it's cancer," I told him. Grampa looked at it and said, "That ain't a cancer . . . that's a ring worm." He said, "Good thing it's July." Then he went over and picked up a walnut. He cut off some of the hull and rubbed that green juice all over my leg. He said to do that once a day for awhile. I took some walnuts home and followed his instructions. Damn, it was a miracle. I couldn't believe it. I had spent a whole year thinkin' I might lose my leg and grampa cured it in less than a week.

Headed for the
Poor House

Gramma and grampa lived on next to nothin'. They were always wishin' and hopin' they had somethin' that was worth somethin'. "Maybe that old Civil War sword's worth somethin' . . . if we could jist find that half-dime, that'd be worth somethin' . . . if that old pocket watch kept time, it'd be worth somethin' . . . believe that pitcher frame there might be worth somethin'." So one day when an antique dealer come through outta St. Louis, they were real excited when she knocked on our door. All the poor people in town let her in. She drove off with a truck load of "old stuff they didn't need anymore." Gramma sold her our coffee grinder fer 2 dollars. They hadn't used it in years . . . they'd moved up to instant crystals. Grampa got him a bottle of booze with the money. That night we turned on the radio and sat in his room and listened to the ballgame. He poured me alittle whiskey and mixed it with sugar and water. The Cardinals were ahead . . . grampa was happy . . . he took another sip from his glass . . . and we talked as we always did about that time we really did almost have somethin' that was worth somethin' . . . that "law suit." Mr. Oliver had started a fire in a burn barrel. We were sittin' in the front yard. There was an explosion and the lid of that barrel sailed across the road at a 1,000 miles an hour. Just missed gramma . . . hit a tree and dug in 3 inches. Grampa banged on old man Oliver's door yellin', "I'm gonna sue you fer all yer worth." Nothin' ever came of that though . . . we didn't even have us a town lawyer. But grampa always claimed that if that lid had cut off gramma's head . . . he'd a found him a way up to the county seat. "Surely to god, you ort to be able to turn that into somethin' that's worth somethin' . . . gettin' yer damn head cut off."

"The Only Thing Worse Than a Preacher . . . Is a Preacher's Son"

Grampa was nearly 80 when he up and decided he wanted to be saved. He put his tie on one Sunday morning and walked down the road to the Baptist church. Dad thought it was just some kind of phase he was goin' through 'cause he'd had him some chest pains. Later after he'd checked out good at the doctor's office, we figured that'd be it . . . he'd be done with religion. But he kept goin'. He'd bring home little pamphlets and booklets on Jesus Christ and how to get into heaven. Sometimes at night me and grampa would sit in his room. It was always dark and musty in there . . . smelled like smoke and apples. He'd turn the coal oil lamp up and we'd drink alittle whiskey. Then he'd read to me. It didn't sound so awful . . . the stuff about god. Dad was mad though. He really resented that grampa went and "got religion." It was almost like grampa had sold out . . . become a traitor. Dad just refused to believe it. He would get drunk and growl, "Ain't nobody connin' him with that crap . . . he don't believe that crap . . . the old man's just bullshittin' . . . that's all he's doin' . . . bullshittin'."

Gramma's Room

Gramma slept on the very edge of her bed (she always had to lay straight like a pencil), it was so piled up with things—crap mostly and junk she'd received through the years. She had a faded yellow wash rag tied up special to look like an angel. It was sprinkled with glitter. It hung on the wall and looked down at gramma and her possessions: an Orlon sweater, still in the box, sent by a cousin no one remembered, pretty hankerchiefs, lace doilies, a set of fancy hand embroidered Irish linen tea towels. There was a bolt of old muslin, some striped mattress ticking, scraps of cotton print, quart jars of bright buttons, a pile of sheets stained and discarded by a neighbor more fortunate, a set of shear plastic curtains, a cigar box full of pens and pencils, and a much prized, never used stainless steel flatware service acquired with Top Value stamp books. Afew paperback books, pamphlets on preserving, seed packets, chicken feathers, coffee cans and rags. Her dresser was just crammed with letters and post cards.

Once my aunts decided to do some cleanin' . . . those fools

74

made a bon fire in the front yard—they took that dresser drawer out, turned it over and burnt every correspondence she'd ever saved for the last 75 years. They didn't even bother to look to see if we really did have that letter grampa always claimed we had—the one signed by Abraham Lincoln.

She Was Drinkin'
. . . Drinkin' Jist
Like a Man

My aunt Ruth was a hot tempered red head. Married and divorced young with a daughter, she was always lookin' for a man. Nothin' much ever worked out in that department. She spent alot of time in taverns and started takin' my cousin along when she was just 13. "Why, she's been guessed at 21," she'd proclaim proudly. I felt sorry for Sandra who was just a chubby girl with too much make-up. As Ruth got older and her fiery hair started coming out of a bottle, her dates became less frequent. Her and my aunt Maudie would come down home to gramma's and sometimes go out to the Birdcage. Once they didn't make it back until real late and the next day there was alot of whisperin' goin' on. "Bastards this" and "bastards that." Somethin' about callin' the cops . . . but no . . . how can you PROVE anything . . . god damn it to hell . . . we ort to call the cops though . . . my whole pay check's gone." Later after they left, I asked gramma, "What's the matter?" "Them boys robbed em," she said. And gramma went on to explain that two young men half their age asked my aunts to dance and once they got them out on the floor, and were waltzin' them around, another boy rifled their pocket books. "Took all their money . . . made em pig of the party . . . pig of the party," gramma yelled. And I thought about Ruth and Maudie and their factory pay checks that they worked so hard for, and I felt bad that those boys would steal their money. I know my aunts were sad. They didn't even "go out" for a couple of nights . . . just worked on a case of beer at home.

Tape Worm

Ruth always said I was so skinny 'cause I had me a tape worm. She said, "You ort to not eat fer 3 days and then hold a piece of raw meat up in front of yer mouth . . . open wide . . . and when it comes up after that meat, grab it and . . . pull it out!"

"Won't I choke?" I asked.

"Naw, you gotta pull it out quick," she said, " 'fore it gets that meat and goes back down."

He Cut His
Own Throat

My aunt Maudie went up to Elgin to get on as a nurses aid. Not much work in southern Illinois so once in awhile, she'd head north. She met a guy up there and within 2 weeks got married. She brought him down home to meet gramma and grampa. He was a rough lookin' red faced guy. Reminded me alot of those men that would come through town workin' the rides down at the reunion grounds. Gramma and grampa liked him . . . at first. He talked about what a good fine cook gramma was and what a good fine gardner grampa was. He even took to callin' them "mom" and "dad." Him and Maudie took over the front bedroom and settled in. One day he had a coughin' fit . . . spit up blood. Gramma was so worried about him . . . gave him croup tablets and prayed he didn't have him a cancer. After that he started drinkin' alot and took to yellin' at Maudie right in front of us. And once at the dinner table he just pushed his plate back and said right to gramma's face "I aint eatin' this damn baloney and beans." He got up and walked out. After a month he started askin' gramma for money. The first time, she gave him a 10 dollar bill. The second time, she refused him and mumbled some stuff about her "fixed income" and the taxes on this place. He went out that night with Maudie . . . they got in real late . . . real drunk. He was talkin' loud and knockin' Maudie around. Gramma got outta bed and reached for her .38. (She always slept with it under her pillow.) She went in there and stood outside their door. She could hear him hittin' on Maudie and that made her mad. Gramma banged on the door and yelled, "Let her alone or I'll cut you in two." Then she fired a shot into the floorboards. Things quieted down and gramma went back to bed. Early the next morning, she told him he'd wore out his welcome. "Don't go," I whispered to Maudie. But she left with him. She came back in a week though with her false teeth in her purse. That no good bum had hit her so hard, he knocked em outta her mouth. They flew across the room, hit the wall and broke in half. "How're you gonna eat?" I asked her. "Oh . . . I'll jist get these welded," she said and she set the busted pieces on the table.

Wedding Portrait

Ruth married her a good lookin' guy with curly wavy blonde hair. He combed it like a movie star. He had on a double breasted suit and a tie. He was smilin' so big. Ruth was wearin' a pretty flowered sundress. She had a straw purse and open toe high heeled shoes. They seemed so young and in love . . . just startin' out. But life didn't turn out like the photograph. All they did was fight. There were so many knock down drag outs. Black eyes, twisted arms, bad bruises, teeth knocked out and my aunt gave as good as she got. She could punch like a man. Sometimes she'd get fed up and leave him. She'd drive down to gramma's. I was there once playin' in the yard when she pulled up. I ran over to the car. I could see he'd worked her over. Her lip was split open and her neck all scratched up where he'd choked her good. I followed her into the house. Gramma took one look at her and yelled, "Lord god, when are you gonna leave that good fer nothin' no account?" Ruth didn't say anything. She just started unbuttoning her blouse. She pulled it back to show us the awful burn marks on her tit. She told us that s.o.b. had put a lit cigarette down the front of her dress and then she said "he pressed it in," like that's what really surprised her. Gramma just sat down on the couch, shakin' her head.

Ruth only stayed afew days that time. Me and gramma begged her not to go. "Don't you all worry," she said, "he won't try anything for awhile. If he does, I'll just bust another beer bottle over his god damn head." And she showed up again a week later after she'd done just that.

Old Man McCullough

Gramma never talked much about *her* dad. She always said he'd died when she was a young girl. But we never found his tombstone anywhere and we looked and looked in both cemeteries. Gramma wouldn't say much because the truth is . . . he hadn't died at all . . . he'd run off. He was an Irish drunk . . . a bum . . . couldn't stand the gaff. Just turned tail and went somewhere. His son had gotten killed . . . crushed in the wagon brake. He was just a little boy barely walkin'. It was gramma and her dad there at home when the accident happened. Gramma was only 8 but she remembers the awful screamin' and cryin' and hollerin' when her mom come back from town. The little boy laid out cold on the bed with a quilt pulled up to his chin. Gramma said for weeks and weeks her dad drank whiskey and refused to eat. Then one day, he wasn't there anymore . . . just like that . . . gone off to nurse his grief. Gramma and her mom moved to town . . . sold their land for 10 cents an acre. Just gave it away. They couldn't stay out there anymore. Gramma quit school in the 3rd grade to help out. They cleaned for rich people and took in minin' laundry. That was one of the worst jobs you could do back then . . . tryin' to beat the coal dust outta somebody's filthy overalls. Gramma never heard from her dad after that. I guess in a way he was dead . . . dead at least to her.

"... Worth a Thousand Words"

We never went out and had us a family portrait taken. We weren't the kind of outfit to waste any money on somethin' like that. Beer, food, a load of coal, that's what dad was concerned with. But once a well to do neighbor woman took our picture. Me and mom and Alice and Ann went over to her house. We sat on her white wall to wall carpet and posed in front of her red brick fire place. Mom stood there next to us in her high heels . . . hiking her skirt up. She sent the photographs to the Hungarian gramma. Mom wrote the old lady that that was our house . . . that we were rich. That we owned the fancy couch and the pretty lamps on the nice end tables in front of the brocade curtains. She said the chandelier hanging from the ceiling was ours. Afew months later, Ralphie got him a paper route and bought a little camera. This time we sat on bare linoleum in our own shack. Our sticks of furniture were junk . . . ill matched and broken. We weren't smiling. We looked like scroungy brats in the day room of some awful orphanage. Mom looked at the photos. She didn't even seem to notice that there was no warm glowing fire place anymore, no neatly hemmed curtains, no bright chandelier, etc. in these pictures. She picked out three exclaiming, "Look how goot mein legs look!" and those were the ones she mailed over seas.

Maybe We'll Get
Something

Even though I'd never seen her once in my life, I loved my Hungarian gramma. When I was little, sometimes at Christmas we'd get a package from her. I was on constant vigil from December 1 on to see if the mail truck was stoppin' in front of our shack. I was always at the window and my heart would nearly rupture with anticipation and glee if he even walked in our direction. If a package did come . . . it meant foil wrapped chocolates filled with thick sweet liquors, little baskets with fancy dried apricots, pretty tins of bright paprika, lebkuchen cookies, almonds, toffees and beautiful hard candies. Stuff you could never get in our town even if you did have the money. It was heaven when gramma sent something. I wouldn't have to lie at school in show and tell. I really would get a pretty ruby necklace and a cymbal clangin' monkey that hopped in a circle.

"My Worker"

Alice hauled him up there everyday for his radiation treatments. One hundred miles round trip—for 30 days. She didn't charge him a penny for gas or wear and tear on her car and she didn't complain. She was nice to dad. But if mom was too slow gettin' ready, she would roar into the house, slammin' doors and yellin', "Don't keep me waitin', lady." Mom would scramble to get her pocket book and trundle out after Alice, who did let her stop at Kmart once to get new glasses. The eye examiner checked her vision and said "any lens can be made for any frame, it only takes afew days." Alice was too mean and impatient to let mom customize her eye ware. She made mom go on and get some awful old man pair that didn't even fit her face . . . just kept slidin' down her nose.

"She Ain't Got Any Business . . . Goin' Anywhere"

Once mom was somehow able to get a brand new fake fur coat outta dad. He just come home with it one day and she jumped for joy. She put it on real quick and waltzed around outside to make the neighbors jealous. It was a long gray swirl coat. The lining was light pink satin and it was printed all over with little black silhouettes of dancing ladies. They were twirling madly . . . everywhere, goin' this way and that way and even upside down. Mom loved that coat. It was used alot in the winter time to cover us up. We'd lay under there at night keepin' warm . . . smellin' hints of mom's dime store perfume. She would put that fur on and walk so proudly down to the corner store just to pick up a can of beans and a lb. of lunch meat. That coat was cut full . . . big at the bottom and that made it easy for Ann to walk up underneath it. She had to do that alot one winter before she turned 6 and started school. Dad wasn't gonna buy Ann a coat until he had to.

"Jist keep her in," he would say. But Ann didn't want to stay in ALL the time. So mom would bundle her up as best she could . . . long pants, 2 sweaters and a hat and out we'd go. They got so good at walkin' everywhere together. Ann under that coat hangin' onto mom's leg. She loved bein' under there surrounded by those swirling ladies. But people sure did look at us. A pack of rag tag kids and then mom prancing along in her cheap fur. I watched everybody turn around when we walked by. I watched their eyes . . . how they looked down and really stared. They acted like they didn't know what to make of it . . . 2 sets of feet comin' outta the bottom of a single coat.

Pennies from Heaven

When Ann was little we didn't leave her out. We always spent some of our bottle collection money on her. But one day she started showin' up with sodies and candy of her own. That happened afew times. She just said she'd found the money. She said it was layin' out side on the ground. Pretty soon we got curious. We asked her where. She took us out and pointed to a tree. She said, "There's always pennies over there." I went to take a look. I started kickin' around in the dirt and I found one. I was so surprised. IT WAS A STEELIE. A 1943 steel penny. I stood there lookin' at it and then . . . my heart sank to my knees. I slammed in the house and ran into our room. I lifted the mattress and reached around for my coin book. I pulled it out and opened it up . . . all the slots were empty. I sat down on the bed. I'd spent years collecting those pennies. That book was almost full. I even had Indian Head pennies and I had a 1909 VDB. I wanted to kill Ann. That penny alone was worth 40 dollars and she'd spent it on a piece of gum.

"Singin' in the Rain"

Everytime it rains, mom runs around like a crazy woman rounding up pots and pans, wash basins, coffee cans, buckets, cut off milk cartons and anything else that holds water. Once I counted 19 receptacles filling up with rain pouring through the roof. She puts them where the worst leaks are and tries to catch most of it but the place always gets pretty much drenched. Drops jumpin' outta shallow ash trays and aluminum pie pans or something filling up too fast or gettin' knocked over. And there's always way more leaks than we have buckets for. It was hell when it rained. Mom screamin' at dad, "Git up St. John . . . git up . . . you haf to see dis mess." Dad just rolled over. The little kids loved it . . . hoppin' around . . . hands out stretched . . . faces up ward . . . singin' songs . . . the rain soaking them as they danced in the living room. But one time, things got down right dangerous. Water got to where it would leach through the walls and soak the down stairs front room ceiling. So much moisture over time weakened the plaster and one evening after a severe storm the whole works gave way. Mom had just been standing there when the ceiling crashed to the floor . . . plaster, Sheetrock, wet gravel and grit everywhere. Broke the legs off the coffee table and sure enough would have given mom a concussion or maybe even broke her neck if she hadn't decided to empty that pan right when she did. Dad didn't get up for that either. But the next day, hands on his hips, he surveyed the situation. He went down to the hardware store and came back with a roll of plastic which sat in the corner for weeks. One afternoon, big black clouds appeared on the horizon. Mom rushed in, grabbed that plastic sheeting and laid it down everywhere and then she said, "Look Landa, I vish I voot haf hat dat sooner." She stood ready with the buckets. The little kids were already dancing.

Sad Smile

I watched dad's teeth turn green and slowly fall out ...
uppers first. He started complain' about a fish bone got stuck up
in there ... in his gum. He pushed on the tooth with his finger
"See that thang wobble?" He drank a 12 pack, tied one end of a
string around the bathroom door knob and the other end
around his left central incisor and just "jerked her out." The
other front tooth fell out about a month later and when he
smiled, it broke my heart. Mom's just started goin' every which
way in her mouth, gettin' long and migratory. Her breath could
stop a charging buffalo. And the infections. Sometimes she
could hardly get outta bed. He cursed her good but he drove her
over there. The dentist pulled so many that time. She got herself new uppers with her cleanin' money. She was so proud of
her new teeth and she tried to smile alot but it didn't look like a
smile ... more like she was just curlin' her upper lip back. I
think mom has three teeth left now. She goes after them dili-
gently with implements like the dentist instructed ... they
anchor the dentures and keep the clicking to a minimum. Ralphie talks alot about how we never had brushes or paste when
we were little. His teeth are snappin' off now ... front
uppers ... molars rottening. "Use a rag," dad would growl if we

asked for a tooth brush. But I do remember once we got a great big old tube of Crest. We all immediately memorized the words on the box and then hopped around the house repeating, "Crest has been shown to be an effective decay preventative dentifrice that can be of significant value when used in a conscientiously applied program of oral hygiene and regular professional care." "Dis ees causing too much trooble," mom says as she grabs the tooth paste. She hid it some where and later yelled at dad, "Vy did you haf to bring dat toot paste, St. John dey hat schqueezed it everywhere?"

Lost Molar

When we were little if we got a tooth ache it was always the same thing. He'd start hollerin': "This is gonna cost me, god damn it." "This is gonna cost me." I remember Ann got a cavity once. The whole side of her face got huge—real swollen . . . he had to take her. The dentist was an old man in Winchester. He must have been 80 and his "tools" older than that. He took a pair of pliers and just jerked Ann's tooth out. Nothin' to deaden the pain. Nothin' said about a filling. Charged dad 12 dollars. And god damn it to hell he paid it. Ann was cryin' and holdin' her face, spittin' all the way home out the window of the back seat. He swung around . . . one hand on the steering wheel . . . and growled through the cig between his lips. "Don't get any damn blood on my car."

"Cain't You Take Care of Nothin'?"

Once I went to the grocery store with dad. It was early December and the place was already decorated for Christmas. We went down an aisle and all along a shelf above the vegetable section they'd lined up some packaged toys. Dolls for girls and trucks for boys. I begged dad to get us something. That stuff didn't cost that much. I could tell. It was cheap junk from Japan. But I begged him. Finally he let me pick out 3 dolls and one of the trucks. We went home and nothin' got wrapped real pretty with ribbon and put under a tree. Dad didn't go for that. He just handed the stuff out. Ralphie ripped the box open and started zoomin' his plastic truck all around the floor. He broke the wheels off right away. Alice and Ann were already markin' on their dolls and cuttin' their hair off. I took my doll outside the next day and started throwin' it up in the air as high as I could. I swung it around till the arms and legs come off. I don't know why we did it but we did it. Dad was so disgusted when he found out. He was mad. He said, "You god damn little bastards, you better never ask ME for anything ever again." We felt awful. We just stood there. We couldn't believe he didn't jerk his belt off and beat the shit out of us . . . we sure had it comin' . . . hell it wasn't even nearly Christmas and we'd already tore up our "gifts."

Tuff Love

We waited 3 days for Ralphie to get up after that one beatin'. Every morning we went in there and stood by his bed and looked at him. "Can you get up Ralphie . . . can you get up today?" He just laid there. He didn't say anything. I hated my dad for what he'd done to Ralphie and I hated myself for causing it. I'd told on my brother. Told dad that Ralphie had knocked over Alice's glass. I didn't know dad would charge in through the back door and hurt him that bad. Dad beat him like he was a grown man. "Stop it . . . stop it . . . stop it," we all cried. He punched him and kicked him and cursed him. He knocked him out and then left. We got Ralphie to bed and covered him up. But no ambulance was called, no report was made . . . no children were taken away. Dad came back drunk later that night. He had him a 6 pack. He didn't even go in there where Ralphie slept. I looked at my dad and he looked at me and then he sat down on the couch and opened a beer. He said, "I hit dat boy too hard . . . I know I hit dat boy too hard." He told me he didn't mean to hurt him that bad. He said he was scared of how hard he'd hit him. He said he wasn't gonna hurt us like that no more. "That wasn't right . . . that wasn't right," he kept sayin'. He drank another beer and then went off to bed mumbling about makin' a man outta that boy . . . come hell or high water. I watched him go and I was thinkin', "I hate you dad . . . I hate you." "You should tell Ralphie you're sorry," I yelled. "You tell him yourself," he said as he slammed the door. I look back now and see that dad didn't make a man outta Ralphie with all that meanness but, by god, he sure enough almost made one outta me.

"They Eat Snails Over There Too"

Sometimes me and Ralphie would go out and try to gig us some frogs. We'd head off down the road to Saline Creek or to a pond we knew about. We were after bull frogs. We took our shoes off and snuck along like Indians. When we got close enough we'd stand up, take aim and throw our spears. Once in a while we'd connect but the commotion would send the other frogs leapin' into the water. So we waited. Sometimes they'd crawl back on the bank and we'd get another shot. The most we ever got was 5. We headed home just thrilled. Some old men were sittin' in the yard with grampa when we got there. They came over to look at our bucket of frogs. "That's a delicacy over in Paris, France," they said, "a real delicacy." We weren't sure what they were talkin' about. They didn't taste like a delicacy to us. They didn't even taste like frogs. They tasted like chicken and that's the *only* reason we liked em.

British Taint

Ralphie had so much trouble gettin' up in the morning after he turned 15. He just couldn't crawl outta bed and get goin'. That made dad so mad. He threw wet wash rags on his face and called him a god damn bum. "Get yer lazy ass up . . . let's hit it," he'd growl. He'd pull Ralphie off the bed and onto the floor. Ralphie wouldn't even know what was goin' on . . . he was out cold. Dad would grab his cover and yell "move it . . . yer goin' to school." It took so much kickin' and hollerin' to get Ralphie to his feet. Finally he'd put his clothes on and stumble out the door. This fightin' and hoorawin' went on for weeks. We were so afraid dad was eventually gonna have to kill him and sure enough one morning it almost came to that. Dad went in there. At first there was no yellin' . . . just a god awful crash. Mom was cryin', "schtop dat St. John . . . schtop dat." I ran in the kitchen. Ralphie was on the floor . . . trapped under the mattress and springs and bed frame. Dad had flipped the whole works upside down on top of him. He was yellin', "You better not be here tonight when I get home from work." Dad left cussin' and hollerin'. I heard him say, "That laziness . . . it's in the blood." We pushed the bed off of Ralphie. He had a big knot on his head. He pulled his clothes on and left. All day at school I wondered about his lazy blood. I wondered if a doctor could fix it. That night dad just laughed and said, "Hell no . . . been in there too god damn long . . . bastards have had it for centuries." He said I wouldn't have to worry. He said it only afflicts the men. He said "it comes from the English side . . . it's passed down." I thought about that and said, "We ain't got that much English in us." "Well, you don't need too awful much to mess things up," he explained. He took another swaller of beer and said, "Shit . . . a little English goes a long way . . . just look at that damn boy."

Ralphie's Tomatoes

Dad was shocked to see Ralphie work that hard on his tomato plants. Ralphie had never helped us much in the big garden so dad wrote him off as a dead beat. Said he was tired of knockin' him in the head to get him to do somethin'. But Ralphie had a class project for the term and he really got goin' on it. He cut off a bunch of milk cartons and grew his plants from seeds. He set em out early and made sure they were covered with plastic if there was a threat of frost. When they got bigger he staked em and tied em up. None of his tomatoes flopped on the ground. He fertilized em and made sure they got plenty of water. Ralphie's tomato plants were the prettiest in town. We made alot of money on them plants and Ralphie got an A in the class. But dad never did give him a pat on the back. I suppose the closest dad came to a compliment was when he growled, "Well, I guess that damn boy can work if he wants to." He said it like he was mad.

"How Many's He Up to?"

Ralphie turned into such an alcoholic. He was well on his way when he was just a teenager. He sure enough learned from a pro. Dad could drink anyone under the table. Ralphie didn't frequent taverns though. He drank at home. Throwin' em back and smashin' the empties in a can crusher. He cashed in the aluminum at 30 cents a pound. He'd just sit there in the kitchen by himself workin' on a 12 pack. One night he went to bed . . . he was so drunk. He didn't even wake up when the cig that fell outta his mouth started smoldering on a chair. It didn't start a fire but it melted into the fabric and completely smoked up the room. He laid there and breathed that awful crap all night long. It took months for his lungs to clear up. He hacked and coughed and spit. He didn't go to a doctor. He just finally got over it the way white trash does.

Tryin' to
Make Good

Once the cops beat dad black and blue and threw him in jail but he wasn't messed up so bad that he couldn't pry the damn door of the cell and escape. He had him a test to take . . . he had to get outta there. He was part timin' it on the G.I. bill and needed a good grade in zoology.

So he showed up bruised and half drunk and sat there with those college kids and took that exam. He answered all the questions and then he went back downtown and turned himself in. The desk sargent kind of laughed when he found out where dad had been and why he'd gone. I don't think they even kept him over night at that point . . . it was just a drunk and disorderly charge anyway. The local paper ran an article in the arrest section and then some reporter from out at New York City called him up. He was a novelty item to them. "Man who escapes jail to take test . . . turns himself back in." Dad told that guy yeah he did get an A on that exam and NO he wasn't interested in no radio show. The reporter explained to dad that the trip would be free of charge. Dad just told the guy that he wouldn't go out to New York fer Love ner Money and that maybe they had time for that kind of foolishness out there but by god he didn't have time for it here. And that was that.

"No Use for
a Dry County"

Between bouts of drinkin', fightin', gamblin' and carousin', dad managed to earn him a Ph.D. He'd started out wantin' to "make a real M.D." . . . but he always said we "came along and loused that up." He kept takin' classes though inspite of us having been born and finally after 15 years up at the college, he actually graduated. Dr. Ralph C. St. John Sr. (Dr. of microbiology). We were so happy and proud and hopeful. He got hired at a research lab and we moved 200 miles north. Dad was able to put a down payment on a fine nice house . . . way too big for the few pieces of busted furniture we hauled up there. He had to drive 10 miles to work in the neighboring town, where he'd refused to live because they didn't sell booze. Dad had picked a little nearby hard drinkin' railroad town for us. Maybe he knew that his good payin' job wasn't gonna work out for long, maybe he knew that our beat up used car was gonna finally give out, maybe he knew that he wasn't gonna ever get anymore offers in his "profession." Maybe that's why dad chose Roodhouse with a dozen beer joints. From where we live, it ain't too far to any of those taverns. A feller can walk it, if he has to, even in the winter time. "Yeah, there ain't no good reason to ever go thirsty."

"Ain't Nobody Hirin'"

Dad wasn't used to the politics of business. Sell outs, take overs, a company "changin' hands." He just figured he'd get a job in the profession he'd studied so hard for and that'd be it. He'd be set. He'd get to do microbiological research and maybe make a difference . . . do some good and for 2 years we were almost middle class. Then one day he came home stunned . . . just shaken. We kept askin', "What's a pink slip? What's a pink slip?" "I've been canned god damn it," he yelled. He went down to the tavern. He could hardly get up the next day. He paced back and forth . . . smokin' . . . shakin' his head. Seems like a new bossman had appeared on the scene. He brought in his own people and cleaned house. Dad wasn't the only one let go. He got on unemployment and typed up some letters and resumes. A place out at Kansas City give him a call for an interview. It was an 8 hour drive but he got in the station wagon. Alice went with him. They got there and finally found the restaurant. Alice said the men were nice and dressed in suits. They ordered steaks and so did she. Dad didn't eat a thing. He just sat there drinkin' coffee and smokin' cigarettes. He told them guys that he was too up set to eat. He said he didn't like to drive . . . it made him nervous. He said he was worried he might

105

have him a conniption fit on the way back. He said that's why he brought Alice . . . so she could "grab the wheel" if she had to. Alice said the men just looked back and for forth at each other. When they were done eatin' they shook dad's hand and said they'd be in touch. Dad and Alice hit the road. They made it home. Finally a letter came. They thanked dad for his time and trouble. They'd enclosed a check for gas . . . and that was the closest dad ever got to gettin' another job in his field.

"Take That Job
and Shove It"

By the time the lab got around to callin' dad back he'd already got on at the local factory. He was so mad that those bastards at Affiliated would fire him like they did and then think they could snap their fingers and he'd come runnin'. He wasn't gonna be pushed around and he told em so. They offered to give him a huge raise. He said he wasn't interested. I guess they thought he was engaging in bargaining tactics 'cause every time he'd say no . . . they'd wait a day and then call with an even bigger offer . . . somethin' he couldn't refuse. But dad wasn't playin' games. He had too much pride to ever think about goin' back to work there. Finally he had to get serious with them people. He said, "By god, I got me a job . . . I ain't interested in you dead beats." And that was it . . . He really slammed the door on the middle class deal . . . we were back to bein' trash . . . back to barely gettin' by.

"Where Would She
Have Gone?"

I never left yer vater. I schtayed vid him. Alot of vomen vould haf run avay." I looked at mom. "He put me tru hell," she yelled. She got up and went into the bedroom. She opened a drawer and came back with a piece of blue paper. She put it down in front of me. I had seen things like this before.

Dear Wife   September 9 1976

You are asleep now. I will not bother you with the details but I had a bad beer at Cliffs tonight. It tasted like deoderant smells. Some one might have put something in it or it might have been in the bottle. I am not sure but if I don't wake up in the morning sue some one for all they are worth. I just took one small sip of it and got another beer in place of the bad one. The beer was Falstaff. I got a good Falstaff in its place and the rest were good. I think I'll be ok.

Love
Dad

"He Might Not of Thought She Was Worth Killing"

Dad would take his fist and put it on mom's forehead and then drag his knuckles down her face . . . pushin' real hard on her nose and her lips and her chin . . . mashin' them. She stood there trembling as he menaced her. Then he would go out drinkin'. He NEVER took her. I don't think he ever took her anywhere. He never bought her a birthday present or a Christmas gift. He never gave her a bouquet of flowers. There was no Anniversary celebration. Once he did come home with a heart box of candies. It was on the kitchen table the next morning. Mom was in a state of shock and refused to accept it. After he left for work, she kept sayin', "Vy . . . vy ees he trying to give me dat now?" We were trilled at the gesture and didn't have a problem with his motivation. We ripped the cellophane off and fell upon those chocolates like starved dogs. We devoured all of it and then fought over the red foil box until we tore it apart. But mom had refused to eat even a single piece of candy. She just stood there watching . . . thinking . . . wondering why he would, out of the blue, bring her a Valentine and then she said, "Dat man must haf done someting wery bad." She swept up the mess we'd made and threw it in the trash.

Balance Brought Forward?

I try to imagine mom's childhood in Nazi Germany. She got separated from her family early in the war and didn't know for years if they were dead or alive. She ended up on a work detail assigned to the fields. A bunch of orphans digging potatoes with their bare hands for local farmers who fed the troops. By war's end, she was lucky to be alive. She had "made it." She arrived in Salzburg and went to work for a prominent family taking care of kids. That's where she met dad, a handsome young soldier who watched her ride her bike back and forth running errands for the rich lady. They fell in love and got married. My brother was born over there. I don't know what mom expected in marryin' a G.I. When she came to America, she saw that the streets were NOT paved with gold. She wound up in a cinder block shack in southern Illinois with her in-laws. A dirty little nowhere town where everybody crapped in an out house. I can easily imagine how mean gramma and grampa were to her . . . unwelcoming, spiteful, cold, angry that dad had gone over there and drug somethin' back. For years, she couldn't even hardly speak English. I know she had it rough, but I know there were alot of other refugees who married soldiers and came to America. Those women tried to make a go of things.

Most of them learned how to drive a car. How to add and sub-tract. How to make a batch of cookies. And maybe sew on a but-ton or even hem curtains. And I try to think about her anger at dad who became an abusive drunken bastard. He totally con-trolled the meager money we had. But then, I get mad and hate mom again and I think, "Hell, even though he never once let her write a friggin' check . . . surely to god she should have at least figured out what one was."

A Red
Letter Day

Mom was always anxious to get the mail . . . like it mattered what came there. Occasionally in her life she'd received afew cards from her relatives with a little money . . . maybe a 10 dollar bill at Christmas time. And once even a check for a 1,000 dollars from her cousin in Ohio. They'd sold the old great aunt's house and I guess, felt sorry for mom. Those people had actually been to our place and seen how we were livin'. But the letters with money hadn't come for years. You'd never know it though . . . the way mom hopped to check the mail box. Usually she'd come back with a hand full of flyers and circulars and maybe an electric bill. Most of the stuff was just junk . . . current occupant crap but she always started pacin' around, lookin' out the window, down the street, checkin' for the mailman hours before he was even due on our block. It was the high light of her day . . . seein' what might come. Lots of time the mailman would just walk right past our house. Mom would be peekin' out through the curtains. She'd turn around and say, "Vel, dat's eet, today." If it was Randy Harp, the regular guy, she took it pretty good . . . not gettin' anything. But once in awhile we'd have a substitute lady. Mom didn't have any use for her. No niceties or pleasantries hollered from the porch. One afternoon we got in from shoppin' and mom ran across the yard to see what had come. She slammed through the front door so mad. "Did you get anything?" I asked her. "Naw," mom yelled, "she didn't geeve me nothin' . . . she never does . . . not ewen a bill . . . dat betch."

"Git Out Dee Nice Kaffee Set, Landa"

I guess mom and dad got married over there in Salzburg sometime in September. That was the month when she always started hopin' for somethin' from dad. Nothin' ever came though. He didn't want to commemorate that. Hell . . . he probably regretted it . . . marryin' her. But how could he know she was nuts back then? She couldn't even speak English. He expected a language barrier but he didn't expect an out right imbecile. One day mom said, "Tomorrow I vont to celebrate my anniwersary Landa . . . I vont to have a party." I just looked at my mom. This was a person who had NEVER had a party. She had no friends to invite, no food to serve and no invitations to send. She was sittin' on the couch. She looked around the room and then proclaimed, "I'm goink to have it like *open house.*" She quickly got up and started dusting and cleanin'. She pranced around so cheerful . . . like she really expected that some one might actually show up.

The Bite Felt
Round the World

Once mom and some neighbor ladies were sittin' out back behind the projects where we lived. It was a hot summer night and they'd drug some kitchen chairs out there . . . tryin' to stay cool. They were laughin', talkin', and drinkin', bouncin' their babies. At first mom did have Alice on her lap but I could tell she didn't really want to hold her. The other ladies were huggin' their kids, kissin' em . . . givin' em a bottle. Mom just put Alice down. Alice didn't like that . . . she fussed and cried with her arms out stretched. But mom didn't pay her any attention. Finally Alice managed to get to her feet. She was balancing her-self . . . holding onto mom's chair. Then suddenly she leaned into mom and proceeded to bite mom so hard on the leg she almost took a plug out of her. All the other ladies just looked as mom screamed and knocked Alice in the head.

Those women didn't know what was goin' on till they saw the red teeth marks on mom's thigh. They just stared in disbe-lief. Mom moaned and rubbed the awful bite mark. Then she grabbed Alice and slapped the shit out of her. Alice screamed and cried and plopped down her diaper around her ankles. No one knew what to say. Everybody just got up and grabbed their chairs. The party was over. We went inside and mom slapped

Alice again and then put her to bed. Alice was standin' there screamin' in her crib. Mom yelled, "You vil be sorry you hot done dat in front of dos voman." Then she slammed the door and went in the front room. Mom was nuts and I knew it. I was only 4 years old. I hated lookin' at her and listening to her curse my little sister. I hated watchin' her. I hated realizing that that night she was officially declaring war on a toddler.

R-E-S-P-E-C-T

Alice got slapped around and beat by mom alot. Mom called her names too: Blumpsen which means fat sausage in German. She also called her mud ball and hog, bad kid and trouble maker. Mom was easily provoked by Alice. Once all Alice did was drag our beat up vacuum cleaner out after mom told her not to. Alice turned it on and went to work. She was playin' house and cleanin' up. Mom charged in there and knocked her down. Then mom went after her with a hair brush, "I hot told you to leaf dat ting alone," she screamed. Somehow, Alice made it out the front door. Mom just stood there yellin', "Kom back her you Blumpser . . . kom back her." But Alice ran off. Mom turned around. She was so mad that she wanted to come after me . . . I could tell. But I was almost 12 then and she knew better. The last time she tried to hit me with a hair brush . . . I just knocked it outta her hand. If she tried to slap me . . . I'd just grab her fingers and bend them back. If she tried to punch me . . . I'd just block her puny fists. I'd hurt her arms as much as I could when she swung at me but for some reason and I'm not sure why . . . I NEVER hit HER, I NEVER punched HER, I NEVER slapped HER. I just never thought it was right to hit my mom but damn . . . she had it comin'.

"It'll Grow Out"

Once mom got a Lilt brand home perm kit at the drug store
and her and a neighbor woman down the street proceeded to fry
Alice's hair right off her head. They took all kinds of stuff out of
a little white box. Pink plastic curlers and containers and packets of awful smellin' stuff that they mixed up in bowls. Alice sat
there so overjoyed that mom was combin' her hair . . . showin'
her some attention. She was grinnin' from ear to ear as they put
on rubber gloves and went to work on her. Mom couldn't read
English too well so she had to rely on that other lady to follow
the instructions. They wrapped Alice's hair up and swabbed on
the crap and then put a shower cap on her head. At first Alice
didn't complain much when her scalp started burnin' . . . but
after an hour she couldn't take it anymore . . . she started
cryin'. When mom pulled the shower cap off . . . curlers and
tufts of Alice's hair came off too. They washed the chemicals off
her head and in the places where there was still hair left, it
looked like someone had burnt it down to about a half an inch
with a blow torch. It was just crispy coarse patches. Alice went
to the mirror and looked at her hair. Mom tried to pat the top
part down. She couldn't even drag a comb through that singed
stuff. I don't think Alice cared how it looked. She studied her

reflection and then just ran out to play. Afew kids made fun of her but that didn't seem to matter . . . it was like she didn't even know how bad her hair looked. She was just so PROUD of the fact that mom had actually tried to give her a permanent. I guess she would have suffered through just about anything to have evidence that mom liked her.

Greene County
Pork Queen

Alice got nominated for the beauty pagent: County Fair Pork Queen . . . her and 5 other girls. The winner to go after the State Fair title and maybe Miss America! She was 17.

Got her a swimsuit . . . a one piece wool knit . . . goldish yellow! And practiced walking in high heels with a book on her head. And come fair night the judges and M.C. and audience watched the girls come out, circle around, line up and wait for their names to be called. And my sister's question was: "Miss St. John, what would you do if your date come over to pick you up and his car wouldn't start?" And Alice unable to tell the truth—unable to cry out "My date? My date? My dad won't let us date, we can't go on dates . . . he won't let us date . . . he's afraid we'll get pregnant . . . my dad would run him off with a shot gun." Instead of screaming that to hundreds of ogling fair goers, she calmly lied . . . "I'd ask my father if we could borrow the family car." I couldn't believe it . . . I just couldn't believe it . . . at that point WE DIDN'T EVEN HAVE A GOD DAMN CAR.

That Wasn't
Worth It

Once Alice wrote a song, dedicated to Ronald Reagan. She actually wrote and dedicated a song to that guy because dad was a Republican. Dad had voted for that old man twice. Alice had such high hopes that Pres. Reagan might like the song (she actually sent it off to the White House). She thought maybe she might get her an award or an accolade. Maybe then dad would like her. Reagan never acknowledged Alice. The secret service probably put her under surveillance as a crack pot or at least on a list of people to be watched. Alice didn't even get a thank you note outta that deal. She made the people who knew about the "song" promise they'd NEVER tell anyone. I guess Alice was embarrassed. I think she was also alittle mad. Maybe she felt kind of ridiculous after all . . . it was absurd writing a song of praise about that bumbling bastard . . . Ronald Reagan. Not to mention his wife . . . the only example she set for the American public was to be a size 2.

Word Power . . . the Power of Words

Alice worked so hard to disguise the fact that she was just plain old white trash like the rest of us. She was ashamed. So first she tried to lose her southern Illinois hick accent. Then she read the dictionary and peppered her conversation with big impressive choices. And damn she was repugnant when she enunciated those words. She just wanted to sound smart. It was absurd though. Once she said somebody should be "remunerated." I looked it up and wondered why she couldn't have just said "paid." She loved to say "expeditiously" instead of "fast." She didn't get mad . . . she "took umbrage." And nothing ever got old . . . it became "superannuated." She liked "consternation" instead of problem. And there was never alot of something . . . there was a "copious plethora." And she didn't say mom hit her all the time when she was little she said "mom smote her with abundant frequency." Shit nobody hearin' that crap thought she possessed exemplary intelligence. They thought she was nuts. One time she discussed her modus operandi. She simply said "words are wonderful . . . you can paint with them." And then she started rendering. I guess she'd been in the D's that day because from her orifice she exuded: disquisition, derogate, descry, dingus and diphthong.

Poetic Justice

Alice tried to have her a literary achievement once. She wrote a poem and entered it in a national contest . . . and by god . . . she won. She was so thrilled to get first place. She didn't care that all the other people who sent in poems got first place too. She was on cloud 9 to be a published poet and she paid alot of money to get that compilation of award winning entries. It was just a paper back booklet that looked like it had been run off on an old fashioned mimeograph machine. So what? There on page 280 was her name and her poem. She brought it down to show everybody. She read it to us with such pride. It went something like this:

THE OLD HOBO
Once a bum walked along the road with white hair
and a beard.
His clothes were ragged and old and then . . .
he saw a book . . . in the grass.
He picked it up with his gnarled hands.
He opened it to a page with a poem which he read.

Then a tear came to his eye.
He put the book in his pocket . . .
He would always have it near him.
Then he smiled and . . .
Started walkin' along the road again.

"They Have Manners
Over There"

After Alice got married to Phillip she didn't come around much. She was busy workin' and livin' her own life. But one time she called up so excited. She said Phillip's great aunt was comin' over all the way from the British Isles. Alice felt so esteemed that her husband's relative was actually comin' to visit. She told mom that she was gonna be bringin' down a very important guest. So mom took a broom and swept our nasty carpet, she got out the dust mop, she washed the windows and she raked the trash outta the yard. She had on her nice dress and best smile when Alice and Miss Watson walked up the steps. Mom just chirped and chattered. She cornered that old lady and showed her knick-knacks, scrap books and brocade doilies sent from the old country. Alice just rolled her eyes and barked, "We've seen enough of this crap . . . let's go to Cliff's." It was one of the last places in town still open for business. It was a dump. Just a smoke filled tavern with a pool table and cheap beer. Not much in the way of food. Only shrink wrapped sandwiches: some kind of processed meat with cheese on a bun. Cliff had him a microwave so in 60 seconds they were piping hot. He just dropped em on the table. No plates, no utensils. Mom wasn't particular. She was so happy to just be somewhere.

She'd been in America 30 years and not once had any of HER relatives been able to come from Hungary to see us. But here she was now, enjoyin' herself . . . visiting with Miss Watson who'd come all the way from London. And we were dining out. I don't know what the old lady expected for supper. She just sat there. Mom ripped open her plastic encased "meal" . . . hot steam risin' up around her fingers. She took a bite and then said, "dat's goot." She drank her beer. She laughed and talked. She flirted with anyone walkin' by. And then she looked at Miss Watson and said, "Dis ees a wery nice place." Alice kicked her chair. She was so mad. She almost knocked mom to the floor. Mom was unfazed. She was hittin' her stride. She threw her head back and joked and carried on and then she exclaimed, "Dis ees die best time I hat ever hat in mein life." Miss Watson just sort of smiled and then got up to go to the bathroom. Alice gripped the table with both hands. She looked at mom and screamed, "Stop acting like such a fuckin' idiot . . . you leave that old lady alone . . . you back off . . . she's not *your* relative . . . she's Phillip's relative and by god she's from ENGLAND."

Hog on Ice

The first time Alice got out of her cage and around normal people was when she went to Physical Therapy Assistant School. She finally realized that none of her kids were gonna be physicians or surgeons so it would be up to her if they were gonna have a medical professional in the family. She was so happy to be embarking on a career that was somewhat *doctory*. She started takin' classes and got pretty good grades.

But Alice never realized that what went at home probably wouldn't go in public. You couldn't just say what ever you wanted to the teachers. You couldn't treat them like you treated mom. You couldn't be rude and hateful. You couldn't correct them all the time in class and act like you were an expert. You couldn't just run around thinking you should already be an instructor in the program. You couldn't get away with interrupting a teacher, and sayin' "Listen lady, I know all about the skeleton . . . By god I know what's connected to what . . . I memorized that stuff." They failed her on the final. The grading was completely subjective. They never told her why and she never figured it out.

She was cryin' on the phone, "They're just jealous of me because I'm so smart . . . I was the best one in the program . . .

the best one . . . this is unfair . . ." And in a way she had a point. But there wasn't one dissenting vote . . . it was unanimous. The teachers had to get rid of Alice. They couldn't take it anymore. They didn't care that she was on the honor role . . . that *personality* just had to go. They weren't it about to let that loose on the public.

Alice's Middle Boy

Alice would show up at the house with her 3 kids. The middle boy was the worst. He'd torment mom. Say things to her. Tear up her stuff. For awhile, mom didn't think she could do anything. She needed Alice, so she had to just "take it." Alice would NEVER discipline her kids. She would never say "don't do that." She'd sit back and maniacally watch mom react while the house was bein' destroyed. This was all while dad was sick—in and out of the hospital and mom who couldn't drive a car or write a check, was at Alice's mercy. For months it was like a cyclone churning through the house every time they came down. Mom there alone—dad off gettin' treatment. And the abuse escalated until once Alice's middle boy went up behind mom when she was bending down and pounded mom so hard on the ass she almost fell over. When she straightened up and turned around he looked her right in the eye and said, "There . . . you old bitch." On that occasion, mom went for him but he quickly ran behind Alice and she shoved mom back screaming, "Don't you touch my son lady." The boy then darted out and just knocked mom's plant off the table . . . whack . . . onto the floor . . . the pot broke and dirt and leaves went everywhere. He quickly scampered back behind Alice. He peaked around her skirt laughing. Mom collapsed on the couch, clutching her tits with both hands, moving them up and down and screaming, "Jesus Christ . . . Jesus Christ . . . Jesus Christ." Alice yelled at mom, "Shut up," then she turned to her son, patted him gently on the head and said reassuringly, "Don't worry honey, I won't let her hurt you."

"She Never Even
Hugged Me . . . Once"

Alice did finally take mom in for her eye surgery but not until after she cancelled the appointment 3 times. She made mom wait to get her cataracts removed. "No big deal," Alice said, "She can wait . . . she's not gonna ruin my life. She always treated ME like shit." And then she hollers that after dad's gone, I need to come back and drag all "mom's crap" out in the yard and get rid of it . . . just auction it all off and sell the house . . . that mom won't be able to live there by herself anymore. She starts yellin' about how she's not gonna do for mom . . . and no one should expect her to . . . just because she lives the closest. And she says she may not even take mom to her follow up eye appointment . . . god damn it. "What's she ever done for me?" I hear mom arguing in the background trying to get the phone from Alice, "Dis ees schtill my haus . . . dis ees schtill my haus!" Then Alice yells, "Back off lady, I'm talkin' to my sister." She screams into the receiver, "I'll let her wander the streets homeless or maybe she will get in a nursing home somewhere, but if she does, I'm not contributing a fuckin' penny. She'll be shittin' herself in some MEDICAID wing . . . you know they don't clean up after the old people there . . . in the MEDICAID wing." I hear her laughing as she finally hands the phone to mom.

She Didn't Even
Have a Scrub Board

After we had the flood in the basement and the washing machine short circuited things got rough for mom. She had to do all our laundry in the bath tub. For years she washed dad's filthy work clothes by hand. She scrubbed and sloshed and wrung his ink splattered shirts and pants till her "arms almost fell off." "Look Landa . . . jeest look at dis," she would say holdin' up her gnarled hands. Her thumbs were all goin' crazy and her fingers were bent and messed up. "I can't do dis no more Landa," she would say. But dad never got her another washing machine. Alice finally did. She had a real nice one delivered from Sear's. She showed mom how to work it and then said, "If we ever get another flood and it's plugged in . . . well you're on your own . . . I won't get you another one lady." Mom was so thankful to have her new washing machine. She took care of it. She was constantly trompin' down stairs to see if she'd remembered to unplug it. Every time it rained she checked to see if water was leakin' in. And believe me . . . the only part of the news she cared about was the weather report.

Once we were out some where and it started sprinklin'. Mom went nuts. "Dat ting might be plugged in Landa . . . I tink dat ting ees plugged in . . . I haf to check eet . . . I jist got to."

Finally we made it home and she charged in and ran to the basement. She came back up the stairs pantin' and heavin'. "Eets ok . . . eets ok," she said. I told her to take it easy or she'd have a heart attack. She sat down at the kitchen table and said, "I don't care if I do haf a heart attack Landa . . . Anyting ees better dann goink back to dat tweesting und wreenging."

Gravy Boat

All of mom's dishes came free in a soap box give away. The single stalk of golden wheat pattern was in DUZ detergent. Every time dad brought a box home, we'd hop up and down waitin' to see what we were gonna get. Eventually mom was able to collect a complete place setting for 8 people. The dinner plates, the coffee cups, the saucers, the desert plates and even a few nice big platters. Then we really got lucky. We got the gravy boat. We really went wild when mom pulled that out of the box. Of course we never used that thing . . . it sat on the counter for years . . . it was a prize show piece. If anyone came over mom would say, "Und dat's our gravy boat." Mom loved it. She just loved having something that only rich people have.

Stayin' Alive

Nearly every Saturday in the summer we were at gramma's. We'd work all day in the garden and then that evening we'd sit around and wait for dad to get home from the Legion Hall. It was the worst part of the day wonderin' what shape dad would be in after 8 hours of drinkin' and gamblin'. We devised all kinds of strategies to keep from havin' a wreck on that 40 mile trip back to our house. We'd play 20 questions and talk to him so he'd stay awake. We wouldn't do anything to upset him. He didn't need to turn around and start hittin' somebody. He needed to keep both hands on the wheel. And then there was the question of gas. We always hoped he hadn't lost all his money. We didn't want to be stranded out some where. So I kept a dollar rolled up in my sock. We even had us a plan for a head on collision. We always kept 2 old quilts folded up in the back. The idea was that just before a crash Alice and Ann would throw one over dad and one over me. Then they'd curl up on the floor board real quick. We figured we could walk away from anything with that safety measure. Or at least if we did go through the wind shield we wouldn't be cut up so bad. Dad never knew about any of our precautions. He'd stagger in the house. We'd say bye to gramma and get in the car. Dad would floor it. I'd look back at Alice and Ann. They had those quilts ready.

"You Kids Jist Go on Down There"

Gramma didn't like us usin' the piss pot . . . specially during the day. "Ain't no reason fer that," she'd say. She tried to make us use the out house. But that was such an awful terrifying ordeal. We had to walk through the back garden to get there . . . through the chickens. The big old rooster was the worst. We were so scared. He used to fly at us, then turn around in mid air and swing out with his spurs. We were so afraid he was gonna cut us to ribbons or put our eyes out. We'd be standin' there at the gate about to poop our pants wonderin' if we could make a run for it. Damn . . . even if you did have a 2-by-4 it was still a nerve wracking and dangerous proposition . . . takin' a crap at gramma's.

Modern Convenience

Once gramma got to about 65 and her arthritis kicked in, she could barely haul water up from the well. Pullin' a full bucket up with a rope was hard work for an old lady. So me and dad decided to dig a ditch and lay a pipe line. He got all the equipment and materials and we went to work. I was mostly along for the ride but I crawled up under the house and helped out . . . I wasn't afraid of spiders. We made sure we dug down low enough so nothin' would freeze up in the winter time and at the end of the day gramma had her a bright shiny red pump sittin' inside on the counter. In a second she could have water in a wash pan. She was so relieved and happy to have that pump. She worked that handle and said, "Now ain't this somethin'?" It was the closest she would ever get to indoor plumbing. My gramma would end up livin' her whole life with out ever havin' her a bath tub, a kitchen sink or a toilet that flushed.

". . . Hardly Fit to Eat"

The Illinois Central Railroad runs up through southern Illinois from New Orleans. In the real old days, before refrigeration, unshucked oysters packed in straw would be loaded down there and shipped north in open box cars. That was our "sea food" from early November through December. Of course we didn't eat them raw or on the half shell. We cooked our oysters. Made "stew" and at Thanksgiving and Christmas, oyster dressing. It was a short lived thing because if the weather was too warm or too cold, the oysters would spoil or freeze. We ate all we could get during "oyster season." I say *we* because I want to remember it so bad but the truth is, I never saw any of that. I was just too little. By the time I came along, things had changed. There was no steam engine haulin' those fresh oysters through town . . . loose packed in straw. I just heard about it alot when I was a kid. Especially from gramma when she was mad and tryin' to make do with clear plastic cartons of "fresh-frozen" oysters from the grocery store or worse yet . . . those "nasty things in a can."

"Goin' to Town"

Gramma always did her tradin' on the ticket down at Wanda Lightfoot's general store. At the end of the month, Miss Lightfoot would open a big box-like contraption that had stacks of everybody's receipts arranged side by side. Metal clamps held them neatly together. Some times gramma could only put alittle on her bill. Other times, she'd square up. I loved goin' to the feed store, walkin' through the back, past the chicks in cages and bales of straw. In the front, they had groceries . . . big old long hunks of baloney. The guy let the slices drop on white paper. Pound and a half wrapped up with string. There were 16 oz. 5 cent sodies. Quart bottles of milk. Sunbeam bread. Pork-n-beans. Cans of soup. Saltine crackers. Just everything you could possibly need. Gramma never got out of her little town much but once she came to our place and got to go to a great big *real* super market. She was amazed at so many wide aisles lined with so much stuff. She checked prices on things she'd never even heard of. Cartons of this, cans of that. She was shocked to see box mixes for biscuits *and* cornbread. Prebaked layer cakes frosted with curly ques. Ready made frozen fruit pies. There were at least 10 kinds of mustards, not just the bright yellow kind Miss Lightfoot carried. Whole fish on ice and lobsters bigger than any bluegills or crawdads we ever caught. I watched gramma marvel at all the kitchen and bathroom supplies and cleaners.

Those products were useless to her. But she was amazed at that little thing that goes in the bowl and turns the water blue everytime you flush. She'd seen it on T.V. up at Ruth's. She said if she ever got her a "tawlet" she'd try those. She really liked the department with all the chewin' tobacco and snuff. She examined those items closely. Different brands . . . different blends. Lots more than just the Mule Plug she chewed. I thought for sure she'd buy herself something from the tobacco section. But she wasn't going to open her pocket book for anything. She'd seen enough. She wasn't happy with their pricing. "Maybe they do have everything under the sun and then some, but by god, these pecker woods are higher than a cat's back . . . they'll not git a penny from me." Gramma stepped on the black mat, the automatic door jerked open and we walked out.

Tuff Enough

I never thought grampa would die. He just kept gettin' better no matter what happened to him. All the fightin' and drinkin' and carryin' on didn't slow him down a bit. That's the way it was. And later when he was old . . . nothin' changed. He'd come back from the hospital with a bottle of good whiskey he'd picked up in Harrisburg. Then he'd get out and start sprayin' apple trees or feedin' chickens or choppin' wood . . . like he hadn't even had him a major heart attack. And that's the way it went forever. But once he went in and he didn't come back. He started starvin'. He refused to eat. He pulled the tubes out. He didn't want an operation. He wasn't even sure what a prostate was. He tried to nod when I walked in the room. Everybody was crowdin' around and cryin'. Gramma kept sayin', "Oscar . . . Oscar cain't you jist come home one more time?" But he wasn't comin' home. I stood there and watched my grampa quit breathin'. I watched him quit not because he had to but because he was ready to. Grampa was nearly a 100 years old . . . still doin' it his way.

"I Didn't Think
She'd Make It Through
the Winter"

Dad went down home to get gramma one Thanksgiving . . .
she was by herself now and wouldn't have cooked anything.
She came through the door just lost in that fancy hand-me-
down dress Ruth had give her. It must have been a size 20. It
was hot pink taffeta with a full circle skirt covered in lace. She
didn't need any jewlry. There was pearls and diamonds all over
the bodice. Gramma's bony chest under a sweet heart neck-
line. She looked like a scare crow goin' to a cocktail party. She
just loved to wear it though . . . the way it rustled when she
walked. She had on her ragged gray sweater and her black tie
up shoes and dark cotton hose. We said, "Hi gramma." She
didn't hug us when she came in. She went straight to the bathroom. The back of her dress was all wet. Me and Alice walked
in there. She had left the door wide open. Gramma's legs were
so skinny under that arm load of shiny pink fabric she'd
scrunched up to her waist. Alice said, "I'll wash those for
you." Gramma dropped her skirt and said, "Naw . . . they'll
dry." Then she laid her scroungy piss soaked underpants
across the edge of the tub and said, "That's the way I do
em . . . that's the way I do em."

A Cop Come to
Our Door One Day

After grampa died, gramma fell away real bad. She was down to just eatin' canned peaches and drinkin' booze. "My heart medicine," she'd say as she grabbed the bottle with both hands. She asked for and we brought her a quart every Saturday when we went down home. She mixed it with sugar and water. She put it in her tea and coffee.

She got so skinny to where she could hardly bring in coal. The fire went out one night in January; a neighbor found her the next morning. Slumped over on the couch, clutching an empty glass. We didn't have a telephone, so a policeman come to our door that day.

"Ralph St. John?"

"Yes," dad answered.

"Maude St. John is dead."

Dad stood looking at the cop . . . "Thank you" . . . "thank you" was all he could say.

Last Respects

Dad fed em all on his allotment. That's the only reason they didn't starve to death in the winter time. His army check came every month and they cashed it. And after dad come home from the military he went down there and give em 20 dollars a week no matter what. Gramma hid it up under her mattress. I don't think she ever spent any of it. We were the first ones down there after she died and we pulled that feather bed back. Damn . . . gramma was rich. Dad gathered up all that money and used it to pay the funeral expenses. Gramma always wanted to be laid to rest in old-fashion rose. She must of said that a thousand times. But when we got over to the funeral home the next day old man Thorton had her in a gray suit. That was awful. But nobody seemed to care. Dad's sisters just kept wantin' to know about their share of the money. What they had comin' from gramma. They said, "There was a fortune up under that mattress." They were arguin' at the grave site. They said, "We're heirs of the deceased . . . We have rights." Dad said, "You ain't got shit . . . that's my money and I'm tryin' to bury my mom."

Remembrance

I was watching those bitches tearing up the place . . . yellin' . . . fighting each other over this and that and nothin'. Each one claimin' to have a more rightful claim to everything— just junk mostly—useless stuff she'd saved—crap she'd collected and things she'd professed to have. They tore that shack up . . . turnin' it inside out. Hollerin'. Each one announcing "my name's on that necklace, she give me that half-dime, that ruby ring's mine" . . . fightin' over things they'd only heard about. It made me sad. I just turned away and then my heart nearly stopped . . . the Gold Bracelet . . . it really did exist . . . the Gold Bracelet really did exist!! In the commotion, it must have rolled out of some box on the table and come to rest unnoticed in the corner on the floor, partially hidden by stuff already discarded and kicked aside. Some how I was able to fight that irresistable urge to just grab it and squeal (like you do when you're walking and see a dollar on the ground). I quickly pushed some books off onto the floor and bent down after them, but I reached instead for the bracelet and slipped it into the pocket of my sweater. Slowly I stood up. I looked around the room . . . no eyes on me . . . and I walked out with what I have of gramma.

Lab Eggs

Sometimes I remember dad would bring home a big crate of eggs. There were so many in that box . . . maybe a 100. We'd crack em open and they'd drop in the pan . . . the yolk always speckled with red. Those eggs were so bloddy. But we ate em. Dad said they were ok. He said there wasn't nothin' wrong with them eggs. He said he got em at a bargain through the lab. But one morning I cracked one and a little embryo fell out. You could see its legs and beak . . . just like a dead baby bird layin' on the side walk. That was too much to take sizzlin' in the skillet. We quit eatin' them eggs. We wondered why dad would bring something like that home to us. Ralphie said, "He didn't get them eggs at a bargain . . . he probably got em for free."

Eventually . . .
He Got His

When we were little, there was a small grocery store down the street from us. We hated the old man who ran it. He used to follow us around.

He watched us like a hawk. . . . We hated goin' in there. Lots of times his merchandise was no good. Like the candy. It could be old or spoiled. I had a chocolate bar once that had nearly turned white. I went back to see if I could get me another one. He said, "Well hell, you ate half of it . . . I ain't givin' you yer money back." One year he sold Christmas trees. On December 24th we went down there and he had one left. We hoped we could get it at a bargain. But he wouldn't budge. He came out and said, "Fifty cents . . . take it or leave it." We took it but we weren't happy. We drug that scroungy little tree home. Nobody said anything. We all knew he should have given it to us for free or at least for a quarter. Then that old man got sick. He started lookin' awful. Now when we went in there he was too skinny to chase us around the store. He got to where he was too weak to even come around the counter. We could have stolen anything we wanted then. We could have robbed that bastard blind . . . and by god we probably should have.

Dad Said He Just Wanted
to Teach Us a Lesson

One cold winter morning dad said he was gonna drive me and Ralphie to school. We were so glad. Not too many kids had to walk in such awful weather and we were just thrilled to not have to be amongst those stragglers comin' in half froze to death. We got ready and out we went with dad. We were livin' in the housing project near the college then and the whole complex was surrounded by metal cyclone fencing. We skipped along toward the parking lot. Just before we went through the gate, dad stopped and said, "See that frozen fence post . . . put yer tongue on it." We hopped over and did just that. We thought it was some kind of fun game until we couldn't get loose. Then we panicked and jerked away. It hurt so bad. Dad laughed all the way to school. Me and Ralphie didn't think it was funny. We just sat in the back seat tryin' not to cry. Finally we got there and dad let us out. We ran across the playground and then Ralphie started tellin' kids how we'd gotten a ride that day. He kept announcing to anyone who would listen, "My dad brought me to school . . . my dad brought me to school." I just watched him. I didn't get it. How could Ralphie be that proud and happy about a stupid ride when our tongues were nearly ripped out.

Necessity IS the Mother of Invention

Ann didn't have any boots when she was little . . . so I made her a pair. I took scraps of cloth and plastic bags and just wrapped her shoes up. Mom kept insisting, "She cain't go out in des vetter Landa vid no boots." And I kept pointin' at her feet sayin', "Mom those are boots . . . good boots." Ann was convinced. She clomped out the back door and down the steps into a Winter Wonderland. We played outside all day. She didn't even notice when kids laughed at her. She was havin' too much fun and her feet were warm and dry. She was 4 years old and didn't have a care in the world. By the time she was 6 she wasn't interested in rags on her feet anymore. She understood the ridicule. She begged dad for some boots. Finally he said he'd think about gettin' her a pair. But before he did he teased her alot and made her cry. He'd come in drunk and say, "Ain't nothin' wrong with them 'boots' Linda's makin' you . . . I don't need to waste my money on store bought."

She Didn't Even Know What P.T.A. Stood For

Dad didn't give a shit about the P.T.A. He didn't go to one meeting . . . ever. But mom did. She'd doll up and put on her best dress and high heels and we'd all walk down to Brush School. We'd sit in the lunch room and suffer through the boring principal and other speakers. Then finally open house. Mom really liked that part. We'd follow her from room to room as she pranced along like a beauty queen . . . flirting and talking loud . . . drawing attention to herself. She'd stand at the refreshment table and eat the treats that other kid's moms had brought. She had no interest in what the teachers had to say. Mom didn't ask any questions or really look around much at our books or work pages posted on the wall. Mom didn't really give a shit about how school was goin' for us. She'd interrupt a teacher mid-sentence. She'd just blurt out, "Deed you try dee donuts . . . dat's dee best donuts I had ever had." The teacher would stand there lookin' at mom . . . her red lips covered with sugar.

Tryin' to Get Home

When I was 10, I was up for the State Championship. I was a broad jumper! My long skinny legs! I had to take a bus way up to Sterling. Dad drove me 20 miles to Marion and dropped me off in the parking lot of the Bar B Q House. Other kids from other towns were there, saying good bye to their parents. Dad just drove away! "Sunday night," I hollered after him. "I'll be back Sunday night." Friday and Saturday were a blur. In my blue gym suit and 2 dollar tennis shoes, I was a nervous wreck and scratched and choked and placed bad. The bus trip home was awful . . . just screaming kids . . . having "fun."

I sat there . . . worried and anxious for miles and miles. Finally the bus turned off the hard road and headed toward the parking lot. It was dark now. Late at night. I was the only one looking around. And I *was* looking, looking every which way . . . hoping he was there. Straining to see our big old beat up '57 Plymouth parked somewhere out there, parked somewhere . . . waiting for me. Bus wheels crunched the gravel . . . head lights bounced off happy parents getting out of cars . . . the driver swung the door open . . . eager kids pushed forward. I sat back down . . . now what, I thought. Summer night bugs screamed.

"... Watchin' Yer Own Back"

Dad's way of tryin' to encourage you before a track meet was to tell you that you weren't worth a tinker's damn. If you were up for the broad jump, he'd say, "There ain't no way yer gonna win ... some little old country girl who's been hoppin' creeks is gonna take that event." Or if you were competing in the 50 yard dash, he'd say, "Hell, you cain't run, yer as slow as smoke off a shit in August." It was hard to go up to the startin' line with such pronouncements from your dad. It was hard to even try when you *knew* you were gonna lose.

Once though, I put everything I had into winnin' a blue ribbon. Dad actually drove me over to the regionals in Christopher. I was so happy he was there. He watched as I started my run toward the sand pit. I flew through the air and went farther than I ever had ... but somehow, somebody else beat me ... by an inch. On the way home dad informed me that I'd really won, that he'd seen them measure that other girl's jump at an angle and that "gave her the distance." Then he yelled, "You should a said somethin', called it to their attention ... gotten you a 1st place." I looked over at him. "Hell, *you* won," he said ... "those bastards robbed you." I felt awful. I didn't know what was goin' on. I hadn't been standing there with dad . . . I didn't see the men measuring jumps. I looked down at my red satin ribbon . . . I held it out the window of the car and then let it loose . . . 2nd place . . . printed in gold. I turned to watch it sail down the high way.

Mr. Hopper

We had us a town queer. His name was Mr. Hopper and he ran the jewelry store. They sold gifts too: figurines, knick-knacks and whatnots. I never liked the guy. He was always unfriendly to us, looked at us like we didn't have a nickel or maybe like we'd even steal something . . . some of his cheap junk. But once he acted real nice to us . . . came out on the side walk and greeted us and asked us to go on a picnic at the reservoir. He'd taken over the boy's and young men's church group and had arranged a "fun afternoon." We said we couldn't go . . . "Our dad won't let us." He just laughed and said confidently, "Oh, I'll give him a call." And sure enough, the phone was ringin' just as we got home. "Dad's not here," I lied tryin' to save him some grief. Alice was out back with dad. He was shootin' at crows flyin' over the garden. "Could we go . . . could we go?" "NO," he growled, "You ain't goin' anywhere with that FAG." Twenty minutes later, Mr. Hopper pulled up in the driveway, the top down on his big red convertible. The car was full of laughing happy teenage boys. He got out and came up the side walk and knocked. "He's here, he's here," Alice squealed. Dad charged in with his shot gun across his arm. He swung the screen door open and almost knocked Mr. Hopper off the porch. He just started yellin' at him, "move it, move it, move it." Mr. Hopper didn't even have a chance to say a word. He just walked, wide eyed backwards down the stairs. He was lookin' at the gun. "You bastard," dad growled, "You ain't usin' my girls . . . now go on . . . get . . . get off a my property." The jovial boys in the car had gotten real quiet, just sittin' there . . . perfectly still. Mr. Hopper got back behind the wheel of his Cadillac and slowly eased it out of the driveway. We watched him solemnly drive away and then head south. Dad stared down the road after them as Mr. Hopper turned off toward the reservoir. "Well I'll be damned," dad exclaimed. "He's goin' on his damn picnic . . . that sure is one persistent queer."

"A Republican . . . Without a Pot to Piss In"

Dad wasn't one to ever make nice with travelin' salesmen especially travelin' salesmen who lied. Why should he have to have his evening interrupted by a knock at the door from some con artist? Usually he would greet them with a simple "ain't interested" 'cause afterall we didn't need no encyclopedias, magazines or Fuller Brush stuff. One time a guy showed up and said he wasn't sellin' anything . . . he said he was "just takin' a poll . . . a political poll." Well, dad liked the sound of that . . . he always liked to talk politics . . . so he let that guy in. The guy sat down on the couch and spread some papers out on the coffee table. He asked dad afew questions. How long was it he'd been a Republican? How was it he'd become a Republican? That's it. Then he showed dad the life insurance brochures. He started tellin' dad about the desperation of a family bein' left alone in the event of an untimely death etc. I saw dad's expression change when he realized what was goin' on. Dad just started pointin' at the door, yellin', "OUT . . . OUT . . . OUT." The "pollster" didn't even know what'd hit him. He tried to call dad sir . . . he said, "Now sir." Dad was in his face, "OUT . . .

156

OUT." The insurance salesman didn't even have time to grab up his brochures. Dad picked em up and threw em out after him as he walked down the steps. Then dad hollered, "You lyin' bastard . . . you should a told me out right you were sellin' insurance . . . by god . . . I need some."

A Stitch in Time

When I was 12 years old, I was relentless the way I jumped up and down and hollered for a sewin' machine. "Please daddy please." Sometimes, he'd just growl, "Go on . . . get." Sometimes, he'd slap me real hard. But I wanted a sewin' machine so bad that even hard slaps across the face wouldn't stop me for long. "I'll save you alot of money, I'll make clothes for everybody . . . please daddy." He'd look up from the newspaper, "Don't make me take off my belt." I'd back away a little from the prospect of a beltin' but I wouldn't quit altogether. "I could fix alot of torn things around here," I'd announce to no one in particular. This went on for months until one fine summer Saturday morning he actually said that he believed we could go down town and see if they had anything on sale. And into Singer's we marched. It was just full of beautiful sewin' machines. "Oh, I like em all," I told the salesman. "I'll take any of these." He talked dad into a portable machine that zigged, zagged and sewed backwards. Dad grunted and groaned and squinted from the smoke of his cig but he wrote out a check and handed it to that guy. I was in a total state of shock but I was able to pick up my new machine and carry it out to the car myself. I plugged it in the minute we got home and I started sewin' at the kitchen table. By midnight I had 2 crop tops, 3 gingham checkered aprons, a gathered skirt for Ann and 8 pot holders. Dad came home with a 6 pack. He opened him one and looked at what I'd made. He grabbed a pot holder and said, "So this is what $200 got me." I knew he wasn't mad though, I saw how he grinned when he picked up one of the aprons.

"Size Ain't Necessarily All It's Cracked Up to Be"

Dad was a real good arm wrassler. Nobody could believe that somebody that short could be that strong. So he took alot of unsuspecting son of a bitches to the cleaners. "Big over grown bastards," he'd say. He was a champion until he was about 55 and then one night he went up against a brick layer half his age who refused to go down. It ended up a draw with that guy but dad's shoulder was so messed up from holdin' his own that his career was effectively over. He never went to a doctor to check on what he'd tore up so bad in there. He had to sleep for weeks with his arm bent . . . his elbow pointin' straight up. He quit wrasslin after that and his arm did get alittle better but it always popped and snapped and he always had to favor it. I still thought my dad was the strongest man in the world though. I remember that time when I was little. He come in from the tavern with his sleeves rolled up . . . his biceps bulging. He picked us up. He hugged us. He was laughin'. He liked to say, "The bigger they are . . . the harder they fall." He was so drunk. He gave mom a 10 dollar bill. He said he won that. He actually said he won that for us.

Behind the Eight Ball

Dad could sure play pool. One year he won the locals and the regionals. He probably would have even won the state contest if he'd had him a way up to Springfield. He thought he might be able to get a ride with someone but that fell through at the last minute. So he just sat around the house smokin' cigarettes the day of the tournament. He drank afew beers and mumbled somethin' about next year havin' him a car that worked, by god. We'd been without one for years . . . since that one night he barely got the station wagon home. It just gave out in front of the house. Dad worked on it for weeks . . . cleanin' spark plugs . . . messin' with wires and filters. Finally he gave up. He'd heard the rumor goin' round the tavern. He came home drunk on his ass, sayin', "some bastard sugared my gas tank . . . I'm gonna have to kill somebody."

But the next day he just got up and drug his old beat up rusted red bicycle outta the basement. He aired up the tires and hopped on it and didn't mention the car again. He went about his business: goin' to work, goin' to get groceries, and goin' to the reservoir with his fishin' poles stickin' outta the back basket. Didn't slow him down a bit . . . not havin' a car . . . at least not till now . . . till he needed to go 50 miles and become a state champion. He took another gulp of beer and growled, "Yeah, we'll git us one . . . we'll git us a car . . . next year." Then he grabbed his pool cue and went out and hopped on his bicycle and rode down to take on the local boys.

Rough Ride

Them pauper bastards back home never fix the streets. Most people though have cars and never really notice the bad roads. Dad was the only guy in town on a bicycle. He'd come home drunk on that thing and sometimes be lucky to make it. Sometimes he'd hit a pot hole and have a wreck. And when that happened if he could he'd just get up and limp down Palm Street. Once the cops had to bring him home. It was so late. Mom was up pacin' around waitin' on him. They drove up in a squad car and pulled his bike outta the trunk. Dad got out of the back seat grinnin' just like a kid. He was all cut up and bloody from fallin' down. He looked like someone had took a Brillo pad to his face. He staggered up the stairs. The cops didn't talk P.D. There wasn't no ticket issued for Drunk and Disorderly. Those cops thought they were smart. They acted nice and concerned about dad. Those fools. They didn't know that they could have done what ever they wanted . . . beat him up . . . thrown him in jail. He wouldn't have sued nobody. He wouldn't have sued the city even if he broke his neck. He would have just blamed him self for bein' drunk and goin' over the handle bars. Dad stood there in the front room. Mom didn't say anything and the cops had to get goin'. They told him Good Night. They even called him Mister. They said, "You be careful now Mr. St. John." Mom was lookin' at his face. She took him into the bathroom and washed him up. It was amazing . . . I couldn't believe it . . . that night she didn't scream or yell or go crazy at all. She just laid him down and put a cover on him.

She Didn't Get Pregnant
That Summer

Dad had always been a maniacal anti-abortionist but because he was such an unaffiliated loner . . . his opinion never amounted to much. All he could do was grumble and vote. He would take mom up to the school house on election day and force her to mark the ticket for HIS candidates. He never picketed or marched for any of his beliefs but at least he was gettin' two votes for the guy of his choice. He wanted to do away with those liberal bastards who were behind the terrible practice of women bein' able to kill their unborn. He figured it was his business to protect all them babies. He'd get drunk and say if we ever had abortions . . . we'd be out. "Don't you even bother to come back home," he'd growl. It didn't take too much to set him off. Like one night Ann needed an application signed so she could work down at the Shawnee Forest. He'd said he'd give his consent but when he looked at that paper and saw that it was a coed program that lasted 8 weeks he went nuts. He said a 16 year old girl didn't need a summer job like that. He said she could just work at the King Freeze again. He said if she was to get pg down there, by god, he wasn't gonna tolerate an abortion. He kept lookin' at that paper . . . turnin' it over. He wanted to know where was the box to check for NO ABORTIONS. "I ain't consentin' to murder." He just got drunker and crazier as Ann waited for his signature. Finally he wadded the paper up and threw it on the floor. Ann grabbed it and tried to flatten it out. She was so upset. She said she wasn't gonna get pregnant and have an abortion . . . she promised dad. She begged him to sign the paper. "I want to go . . . I want to go," she cried. He just crumpled his last beer can and staggered off to bed. When we got up the next morning, the application form was on the kitchen table and we were so shocked . . . HE'D SIGNED IT. Ralph C. St. John Sr. and in the blank empty margin on the left hand side of the page . . . he'd created his own category. He'd scrawled in big wild letters: NO ABORTIONS! Ann sent the form just as it was.

Treasure Trove

I was sittin' on the couch with mom when she picked up that great big old shell we'd had forever. It was the kind some people drill a hole in and turn into a novelty lamp. "Listen to dis," she said as she handed it to me. I put it up to my ear. "Dat's dee ocean Landa," she announced. "Oh yeah, I hear it mom," I said. She quickly got up and grabbed a basket. She started scamperin' around, gathering up all the shells she'd ever found, collected or been given through the years. They were stuck here and there around the house . . . in flower pots, in ash trays, in candy dishes and tied up with red ribbon hanging on the wall. "Dey are all singing Landa," she said as she set them on the coffee table. "I just heard it von day . . . dey are singing . . . singing vid dee ocean." She sat back down and proceeded to pick them up individually, listening carefully to each one herself before passing it on to me. She'd smile and laugh and exclaim, "See dis von . . . dis von has it too." I looked at my mom, like a child, exuberant about some new incredible discovery and I said to her, "How do you figure the ocean can still be in there?" "I don't know Landa . . . I jist don't know," she said as she handed me the last shell. It was so small but sure enough, the ocean crashed and roared inside its tiny pink curves. "Mom, have you showed these to anyone else?" I asked her. "Oh NO Landa," she exclaimed as she arranged the shells, "I can't do dat . . . I can't take dat chance . . . vee haf to keep dis a secret . . . or some von may try to schteal dem!" She looked over at me and said "Don't tell nobody . . . vee may haf to sell dem some day." Then she shoved the basket up under the couch.

"The Birds and the Bees"

I didn't think I would ever start my period. I was 15 before it happened. The 1st episode I didn't tell anyone. I just handled it. The next time mom saw the sheet. She pulled it off the bed and said, "Vel Landa, you are a voman now und you can geet pregrant if you geet raped." I had never heard it put quite that way before in Health class. I just looked at her. I said, "Ok mom . . . I'll remember that," and I headed off to school.

We Didn't Fall
for That Crap

When we got alittle older we treated mom as bad as she treated us. We didn't give a shit if she liked us. We knew she couldn't like anyone . . . so what the hell. We let her have it. We called her names and back talked her and totally disrespected her. Some times she'd erupt in crocodile tears . . . moanin' and Jesus Christ-ing and goin' crazy threatening to kill herself because of us. She'd say, "I'm goink out to the reservoir Landa und valk een." I'd jump up and run to the closet real quick. I'd come back and say, "OK, mom, here's your coat." That made her so mad. Once I even said I'd give her a ride out there to save her some time and trouble. Boy, she could turn the tears off like a faucet. It was an insult to us when she made those threats. We weren't buyin' her bullshit. We all knew mom wasn't about to kill herself . . . she didn't have sense enough to kill herself.

"Big Red Slicers . . . 6 fer a Quarter"

We didn't beg when we were little . . . we just went door to door sellin' things . . . stuff we'd made. We'd canvas the rich neighborhoods, go down streets that had big houses with grass in the yard. We'd look for two car garages and tall T.V. antenaes. And if there were pretty flowers planted here and there it usually meant a nice lady would open the door. We'd knock and stand there . . . 3 little girls in ragged dresses and worn out shoes. We had all kinds of special home made things at good prices. One lady bought all the little yellow clay chickens I'd made at school. Another bought the seals. They were black and white spotted—it was a set. A mom and 2 babies. The ladies usually gave us way more than we asked for. We sold little cloth books, embroidered hankerchiefs, and little pins carved from wood. But mostly in the summer we sold vegetables. We'd start early in the season makin' the rounds with radishes and leaf lettuce. Tomatoes and roastin' ears were our biggest sellers and finally in the fall, we'd pull pumpkins all around town in a red wagon. Little sweet sugar pumpkins for pies and great big old Jack-o-lanterns for carvin' at Halloween. Some of em weighed at least a 100 pounds. We had quite a reputation with our home grown produce. People just loved to buy our vegetables. Even years after we gave up goin' door to door, I'd be walkin' some-where and some old lady would recognize me and holler out the window, "Yahoo . . . yahoo . . . girl, you got any okry . . . gonna have any cull tomatas fer cannin' . . . yahoo?" I'd just ignore her. I was 16 by then . . . had me a real job at the Bar-B-Q Shack. I'd pretend I didn't know what she was jabberin' about. I'd turn my head away . . . how could I let the popular boy holdin' my hand know what kind of trash I used to be?

"It Takes One
to Know One"

I hated the way mom always called me a whore. I wasn't doin' anything wrong. I was 16 and out somewhere with my friends. I'd come home and bang on the door. She never let us have a house key. We had to wake her up. She'd open the door yellin' and hollerin'. I knew it wasn't that late . . . I always got in way before dad . . . I wasn't stupid. I'd just push past her. She would be screamin', "Ver haf you been you whore?" Sometimes I wouldn't even answer her. Sometimes I'd say, "Don't knock it till you've tried it." That drove her crazy. She'd stand there in the dark and call me names and mumble the "Yer vater's goink to beat you goot" crap. I'd just go to bed. That next year after she found out that I'd got knocked up she thought I'd proved her right. She said, "Dat's vat you geet Landa ven you schlut around." I screamed at her, "None of the *sluts* in high school are pregnant . . . the sluts don't get pregnant . . . they know what to do mom . . . you stupid idiot."

My Pregnancy and
His Existentialism

We hit the railroad tracks goin' too fast and damn near hot boxed. The muffler was draggin'—shootin' sparks. I was in the back with Alice and Ann. I was thinkin' about George. "Vel, ver ees he today?" mom asked sarcastically, not sayin' his name. I didn't answer. I knew he was at his mom and dad's, layin' around in his bedroom, smokin' a Camel cigarette, thinkin' about existentialism. Reading *stupid* books! I looked out the window. We were gettin' into town. People on the sidewalk turned to look at us . . . white trash in a beat-up old rusted out '57 Plymouth Savoy. I wondered if he would call me. I wondered if his mom had made his favorite pie. I wondered if I would see him that weekend. I wondered why he didn't want to hold my hand anymore. Dad pulled up in front of our shack. My sisters ran off to play. I went inside to wait by the phone. He lived across town in a big house. They had an upstairs, a nice yard, a new car, wall to wall carpeting and top sheets on the bed. But he still liked me anyway—he loved me. Well . . . before I got pg, before I started wearing the same dress everyday, before he started checking out all those books by a guy named Nietzsche. I tried to comprehend the "uselessness," the "absurdity," the "nothing matters philosophy" he began to sub-

174

scribe to as his calls to me became less frequent. Finally, I just dialed his number . . . "Hello George, Happy Thanksgiving," I said. "I'm busy, I'm reading," he yelled. "Oh . . . ok . . . well, call me," I said. "Yeah," he replied and hung up. I went outside and sat down and tried to stop my tears. Mom walked out on the porch and stood there. "Landa, are you pregnant?" she barked. I wiped my face, looked at her and said, "No mom . . . are you?" She walked back in and let the screen door slam.

2nd Blood Test

By December, I was pretty far along. I was way past trying to get my blue jeans closed, and pretty much down to just wearing that striped A line knit tent dress. I could just barely button my coat. I put on a head scarf and rubber boots and that's how I set out that afternoon. This would be my 2nd long walk out to the clinic on the edge of town. My 1st blood test had expired because George was too busy to go over to the court house with me. It was cloudy and cold that day as I walked along the hard road and people were looking at me as they drove by. When I got there, I went up to the front desk and said, "I need a blood test to get married." She directed me to the lounge where I sat and waited before. "Linda St. John," a nurse called out after awhile. I went in a small room and the same doctor came in. He drew blood from my arm and sort of looked at me. "Weren't you the girl in here last week?" he asked. "Yes," I replied. He filled out the form. "Here," he said laughing as he handed it to me. "Maybe he'll marry you this time."

Wanted: Live in Babysitter—Pregnant Teenager Ok

I'd read the ad in the Chicago *Sun Times* and I quickly called the number. I didn't have any choice, I could tell that George didn't like me anymore. So at midnight I caught the Illinois Central and got up there about 8 o'clock the next morning. The lady sure enough knew me . . . picked me right out of the crowd. She was hard and rough lookin' . . . said she was tired, had just got off the grave yard shift at the factory. We took off in her beat-up old station wagon and she didn't say much . . . just that she'd already found a girl but would help me anyway. When we got to her house her kids jumped up and down . . . "Mommie . . . Mommie," they squealed. She hugged and kissed them. I stayed there several days. She fed me SpaghettiOs and hot dogs and never asked for a penny. Finally a connection was made . . . an older lady who'd adopted a newborn. Off we went in the station wagon. I felt so scared . . . so alone . . . no one knew where I was . . . I hadn't talked to George in weeks. I started cryin'. She looked over at me. "Honey, don't you worry," she said. "You've got to think of yer baby . . . if you git down . . . you gotta git right back up . . . when I feel like killin' myself I jist go wash my face and then put on a little make-up . . . *always* makes me feel better . . . try it!" she said as we pulled up in front of a little house similar to hers. I got out and watched her drive off. I picked up my suitcase and walked up the stairs to meet the new stranger, hoping she would be a nice lady too.

She Liked to Say, "The Baby Has Mike's Eyes"

She was ok but her husband was always lookin' at me. He was a little small man who never said much. He left early every morning. She said he worked in a can factory. He'd get in after his shift and put his lunch pail on the table. He'd sit down and then she'd hop around and make him a sandwich and open him a beer. She'd try to fuss over him but he just ignored her. That's why she adopted the baby . . . she thought maybe they could be a "family." She was so big and fat . . . nearly twice his size. One evening she whispered to me, "Make sure you lock your room at night in case Mike tries to get in there." I just looked at her . . . I didn't say a word. I knew I had to get goin'.

Swizzle Stick

Some two-leg s.o.b. put a swizzle stick in dad's bottle of beer when he was takin' a piss. He come near chokin' to death in the tavern but gagged and flopped around like a chicken, until, somehow, he got it down. Months later, it punctured his gut. My little sister was cryin' in the neighbor's phone "Linda, Linda please come home—Daddy's swallered a sword." I came back. I was about 5 months pregnant then. I went straight to the hospital from the bus station, and he was up, stompin' around the room. I looked at all the stitches on the huge incision in his belly.

"Hell," he said, "I just done 50 push-ups . . . I got to get outta here . . . I need a drank."

Dirt for His Worm

The 2nd time I ran off I made it up to Waukegan to the Great Lakes Navy Facility where my brother was in basic training. Ralphie was a radar man and Patty was a clerk typist somewhere on the base. She was pregnant too . . . a couple of months further along than me. She would come home frowning . . . mad. She was so unfriendly she never talked much. Just went right in the bedroom and closed the door. Ralphie tried to get supper: hot dogs or hamburgers. When they were at work I'd get in the ice box and have me a Kraft single on a piece of white bread with a little mustard. I felt guilty eatin' their food.

I'd only been there a week when Ralphie started sayin' things like, "This apartment ain't hardly big enough fer two," and "People need their privacy." I refused to take the hint. I didn't have anywhere else to go. The next night Ralphie dropped the tactful strategy and just said, "I don't mind you bein' here but Patty don't like it . . . she said, 'Three's a crowd.' " I just sat down on the couch. He said, "If you don't leave, Patty said she'd 'cut me off.' " I wasn't sure what that meant at first. "Cut you off?" I asked. "Yeah," he yelled, "You know . . . not give me any . . . not put out." I collapsed inside

181

when I realized what he was sayin'. The next morning I packed my suitcase and got on a bus. All the way back to southern Illinois I thought about my brother and I was so sad and disappointed and scared to know that somehow all he'd become was a grown up.

I Got My Ring
at Kmart

When I got back to town, dad didn't run me off. He let me stay there. Me and George went over to the Court House in Jackson County and the Justice of the Peace married us. George dropped me off back at mom and dad's . . . we didn't have us a place to stay yet. It was January 8. It was so cold that day, there was lots of ice on the streets. I got outta the car . . . I was so pregnant . . . I lost my balance and slipped in the road. I went down like a hundred pound bag of potatoes. My feet just went one way and I went the other. I flopped down so hard I almost cried. George had already taken off. Somehow I was able to get up and make it in the house. My hip was bruised so bad. I just laid down. I thought I might lose the baby. I thought George would sure hate that timing . . . for me to have a miscarriage the same day we "had to get married."

War and Peace

Ralphie went AWOL after just afew months. He did somehow manage to make it through boot camp and basic training and dad did actually hug him when he came home on furlough. But once he got out to San Diego and had to face a big old boat, things changed. He just couldn't go aboard and off it sailed without him. He hid out scared in their little apartment and made Patty answer the phone. Some big old harsh military man's voice booming "This is a criminal offense of a very serious nature . . . etc." Pretty soon, Ralphie called us saying if he just had money for a plane ticket to meet the boat in Hawaii he could stay outta the stockade. I put in my tip money and dad got up 200 dollars. He wired it out there and started drinkin'. He talked about how he'd joined the army at 17 and was proud to go. And even though he had one arm shorter than the other he went over seas and fought those krauts. And then every other sentence was "that damn boy this and that damn boy that." Cursin' him. A week later we got word that Ralphie had been given a medical discharge . . . something about claustrophobia. Dad threw that letter down and said "he's as useless as tits on a boar hog." But this was good news for me. I was *so* glad he wasn't goin' to Vietnam. I knew he wouldn't have ever made it back alive. But dad didn't see it that way. And he started calling him a draft dodger and a coward and a bum. "He ain't got what it takes," he growled. Finally I just said, "Ralphie's not a bum . . . he just can't kill people dad . . . he's different than you." (Dad took that as a compliment and went on drinkin'.)

His Car

George couldn't get out of bed in the morning. He just wouldn't get up. Layin' there till way in the afternoon. I was out of food and knew he didn't want me drivin' his car but because he was still sleepin', I thought I could sneak off and go get groceries. It would only take a minute. I got back—no problem, and started cookin'. He finally crawled out and started grumblin' around the house. He went outside and then came chargin' back in. I was in the front room by the closet. "My car's been moved . . . my car's been moved." I didn't say a word. "Did you drive my car?" he screamed. "I told you not to drive my car." I backed away. He pushed me up against the door and grabbed me by the hair with both his hands. He started pounding my head against the closet. Bang . . . bang . . . bang. The nail hooks sticking out of the door were digging into my scalp. Bang . . . bang . . . bang. When he saw blood on his hands, he stopped. He went outside. I ran to the kitchen and put my head under the faucet. I was sittin' at the table tryin' to dry my hair with a towel when he walked in, stared at me and growled . . . "I'm hungry."

Punch in the Gut

When we lived on Michael Street, only a block from the tape factory, George took to comin' home for lunch. I'd fix him whatever I could—what I thought he'd like. Sometimes, he'd get in late and once his food was cold. His tuna casserole with potato chips on top. He knocked me around for that. He threatened to "take care of" me by punchin' me real hard in the stomach so I would lose the baby. I just looked at him. I felt so awful, I didn't care what he did. He threw the plate on the floor and went back to work. When I told my little sister, she came over the following evening and insisted on hiding under the sink so she could jump out and help me if he got mean. Finally he roared up in his Studebaker.

Alice quickly pulled the door of the cabinet to. He sat down at the table and I put the *hot* food in front of him. He didn't say a word, just glared at me, ate and left. Alice crawled out from under the sink and exclaimed, "I'm glad he wasn't mean to you Linda . . . I bet everything will be alright."

.22 Pistol

Livin' in that little blue trailer on Rt. 51 south was the worst. I was stuck out there 10 miles from town. I would wait every night for George to come home. Often, he wouldn't show up till 3 in the morning, which didn't seem that odd to me. I thought all men went out every night carousin', carryin' on, drinkin'. George liked to drive around after his shift at the factory. Cruisin' in the black Studebaker Golden Hawk his dad had bought him. Listening to the radio, speedin' around rural southern Illinois. Not wanting to come home.

He had said the day before that I was fat, that my legs were ugly now, all swollen around the ankles. I was now 7 months along and hadn't been to a doctor yet. It didn't even occur to me to go to a doctor. Stuff was just happening. I didn't know what, if anything, was ahead for me of *my* chosing. I was feeling worse every day. I went to the top drawer and pushed the socks aside. I took out the .22 dad give me. I sat down on the edge of the bed. I started to cry. "I'm done with this," I said. "I'm god damn done with this." I put the gun up to my head. I had nothing to lose. I was cryin', with a baby kicking in my belly and a gun to my head when George walked in. "What the hell are you doin'?" he screamed. I just sat there. He ran over and grabbed the .22.

"Give me that, I don't want the blame for anything like this," he yelled. He took the bullets out of the gun and flung them out the back door of the trailer. They bounced into the wet grass. He threw the empty gun on the bed and hollered, "You're not going to kill your damn self here."

Baby Suzi

I was in a room with a woman whose husband was there all through her delivery. Her friends and relatives crowding around her and her baby the day after and occasionally looking over at me alone in my bed. No one came to see me until the next evening. Dad and Alice. They marched in with a bouquet of irises picked in the vacant lot next to our shack and a box of chocolates bought at the dime store. Alice with tears in her eyes. She'd fought with the lady down stairs at the front desk who knew she was only 14 but finally let her come up anyway. I was so happy to see somebody. Dad kept talking about how that old nurse knew she couldn't stop Alice, 'cause by god she said she was comin' through. He really liked that and laughed. Nothin' much else was said about anything. "How you feelin'?" "Ok." "When you comin' home?" "Soon, I hope." We ate some of the candy and I smelled the sweet fragrance of the flowers. Just before they left, the nurse brought Suzi in. She was so little and all wrapped up in a white towel except for her face. "She looks like a doll," my sister said. Dad just smiled at her. "Look at them brown eyes," he said. "Why, that baby's perfect."

Ann Got
Too Busy

Ann backed away alot from the prospect of doin' for dad at the end. She put it on her 3 screamin' brats . . . how she had to take care of them. Who could blame her. Ann was only 11 when Suzi was born and they were brought up side by side. Dad made it plain though that he favored my daughter. He'd take Suzi out shoppin' and let Ann tag along. He'd get Suzi a big pile of clothes and if Ann was lucky . . . a pair of sox. It made her mad and hurt her feelings. But she was never mean to Suzi . . . she knew it wasn't Suzi's fault. And now about dad . . . like visiting or doin' anything to help him . . . well, Ann would say, "I have these guys now . . . they're *my* priority." She really liked that . . . sayin' she had her a priority. I guess that would be as close as she would ever get to bein' one.

Singles' Dance

After her divorce, Ann would dump her kids on mom and go out out bar hoppin'. She pursued that with a vengeance. She got married as a teenager and, by god, now she was gonna enjoy her freedom . . . the fun party times she'd never experienced before. Her and her girl friend from the gym would rat comb their hair up real big and put on their pink short shorts.

She met alot of men and had alot of drinks bought for her. She "took up" with quite afew but nothin' worked out with any of "those jerks." Some she brought home unexpectedly and sleeping arrangements would be altered for privacy. Somebody carried to the couch . . . somebody carried to the back room. Kids waking up, rubbing their eyes, wondering how they got where they were and then a man coming out of my sister's room.

Once a guy refused to displace the kids . . . said he "jist didn't feel right about it." And the next morning, the kids walked through the living room . . . passed a stranger snoring on the couch. They got their bowls of sugar coated puffs and turned on the T.V. The guy woke up and was actually nice and friendly to them but he didn't "work out" either. He told Ann to feed them better food and not all that processed junk. "He's nuts," Ann said. "Bastard won't even eat *chocolate cake,* he said there's more chemicals in cake than in all the dope he took in 'Nam . . . fuck that drug addict."

Cold Morning

Ann's youngest son Dewie was a sweet little boy. Sometimes, he would sit in the corner for hours and play with a fuzz ball or maybe he would draw a hundred race cars on a single piece of paper. He never hollered for the latest toy and he was never in the way. But mom *had* to pick on some one and because he was the middle child or maybe because his hair was yellow or his eyes blue, she chose him. Decided he was the "bad" one . . . a trouble maker . . . the one who needed his little face slapped hard with her open hand. "Get them up," Ann said as she went off to her job at Wal-Mart. And mom would try to get them ready for school. "Eet dis food, git yer shoes, find dee sox, vash yer face, don't schpill dat, do dis, don't do dat . . . you haf dee devil in you" . . . and she starts hitting him, always in the face and he gets up and manages to get away. He runs out and he's on his little bike . . . riding off. He looks back and she's in the door way yelling, pointing her finger at him . . . "Someday somebody ees going to schlapp all dee meanness outta you." And he peddles faster and for the 2nd time in one week when it's 20 degrees outside, he arrives at school early without a coat . . . just blue jeans and the tee shirt he'd slept in.

194

"It Was Fun . . . We Had the Time of Our Lives"

Because she insisted it was a school requirement for one of her classes at the community college, she was able to make mom watch the kids without too much fuss. "Dis ees part of her schkool," mom said angrily. But surely to god, mom saw through the charade because of what Ann had packed: hair spray and short shorts, not a single book! Her work out partner pulled up in a shiny little red car and they flew outta there, chasin' a wild week end. They were single and "fun-loving" and wound up in Nashville. They cruised the bars looking for the best spots. "Boys and booze," they laugh, the radio blarrin'. They screeched to a halt by a big white Cadillac parked on the street and ran up to the driver waitin' behind the wheel and in their cutest, chirpy, little girl voices ask in unison, "Will you take a 'pitcher' of us by yer car . . . we have a camera?" The guy got out and they posed standing on their tip toes, hands on their hips. "Thanks," they giggle and wave as they speed off. And after much debate, and consideration they decide to "crash" the country music D.J. convention at the Holiday Inn.

Lots of fat bald old men turned to see them clomping through the lounge in cowboy boots, hot pants and stretch lace muscle T's. "We're from L.A.," they lied.

"We're professional body-builders." Every old fart in the place wanted to buy them a drink. Wanted to get to know them. But one guy in particular kept hanging around and then started telling the other guys to "back off, the 'girls' are with me." The "girls" just giggled. After afew more drinks, he said, "Can't chose which one I want . . . I'll take you both." Ann narrowed her eyes at him and said, "WHAT?" "Yeah, I'll take you both." "We're leavin'," Ann said. The guy grabbed her arm and growled, "Yer leavin' with me." She jerked loose and yelled, "Fuck you."

"I bought you 'girls' drinks," he said. Ann and her friend were out the door. The guy followed them yellin', "Git yer asses back here." He was gettin' loud and had to be restrained. Some other men grabbed him. "What's a matter with them bitches?" he screamed. "What's a matter with them whores?"

"They Know
I Love Them Dearly"

Ann wanted to make something of herself so one day she ran off to Phoenix. She left her 3 kids behind. She called once in awhile. They cried and fought over the phone. She was just on cloud 9 though with how beautiful the desert was and how spiritual she felt. She just loved the Healing Arts. She said she was workin' on her massage degree. She said she'd see them soon. Mungo was only 5. She would just listen and never say a thing. She only wanted to hear her mother's voice. She held onto that receiver! The boys had to jerk it away from her and she just screamed and hollered when they pushed her aside. Dewie was 9. Neil was 11. And pretty soon, they got to where they hated hearing Ann's dumb incoherant ramblings about energy balancing, cosmic transformation, deep tissue work, dream catchers and soul retrievers. After awhile they didn't even want to talk to her. They got tired of the sleepless nights alone in their room with the dresser pushed up to the door 'cause their dad worked the swing shift down at the factory and couldn't afford a babysitter. They'd had it with her parapsychological mumbo jumbo about the presence of celestial beings. They didn't see any guardian angels around late at night when they were hidin' up under their bed . . . barely breathin' . . . waitin' on day light.

Boys Are People Too

One morning when I was at Ann's, her son Neil got up and belligerently decreed: "I'm 9 years old and I've minded long enough . . . I'm never gonna fuckin' mind again." And then my sister said, "Pick up yer sox." "No." "Pick up yer sox." "Noo." "Pick up yer god damn sox." "Nooo." And then she grabbed him . . . bang . . . bang . . . bang . . . his hard little skull cracked the Sheetrock. And one time I said clean up the yard and he threw trash everywhere . . . the little bastard . . . I strangled him good fer that. Back then, that's the way it was. But today, beatin's are not popular. No more jerkin' the belt outta yer pants, no more goin' out and cuttin' a switch. Ann had heard about this and got herself some "New-age" books on psychology . . . "tough-love," they call it. And when she was finally able to bring Neil to Phoenix, she tried some on him. He was, however, 13 then and not into ceramic angels, clogged chakras, or crystal mineral therapy. And he didn't understand all the men coming through the apartment to get their massages on the contraption she kept in his room. That pissed him off the most . . . what she might be doin' in there. She would close the door and come out an hour later. "Would you like some lunch,

Sweetie?" she asked as she walked through the kitchen. "Sweetie . . . would you like . . ." "No, ya fuckin' bitch, I HATE you," he yells, jumping up from the couch. "FUCK YOU and these stupid angels" and the knick-knack shelf crashes to the floor . . . wings and halos bouncing everywhere.

"I Did the Best I Could"

After so many years of dad treatin' us bad, we just accepted that that's the way he was. We wanted him to like us. But he was always so mad and drunk. There just weren't many nice words in our family. I guess the closest we got to a moment with dad was when he'd sign our report cards and instead of beatin' us, he'd say he "reckoned that them marks didn't look all that bad." Once when Ralphie was a senior he started smokin' cigarettes and got big ideas about droppin' out. Dad said, "God damn ya . . . you think you ain't gonna graduate high school . . . well, I'll tell ya what . . . we're both goin' in a room and one of us ain't comin' out ALIVE." The next day, dad drug Ralphie over to the principal's office . . . threw him through the door and said, "My son's back." And once when Alice was elected for cheer leading in 6th grade, dad refused to buy her the outfit. The other kids took up a collection . . . charity for the lucky girl from the wrong side of the tracks. And the best Ann got was to be ignored and neglected. He was nicest to me of all of them but I rememember the hard knocks and meanness. Some how though after I had my daughter, we saw a whole new side of dad that we couldn't believe. He couldn't do enough for baby Suzi. He bought her things, took her places, remembered her birthday. He talked to her . . . held her on his lap. He NEVER slapped her across the face or beat her with a belt. We watched it unfold and we loved Suzi but in a way . . . we were just devastated to see that our dad *was* capable of kindness.

Suzi's Tricycle

Ralphie, Alice and Ann decided it could be a generational thing with dad. At least that's what they hoped it was. They figured because he loved Suzi so much maybe he'd like their kids too. They'd all come down with their brats and watch and wait to see dad's reaction. Ralphie gave up after the canned corn episode. He was devastated when dad grabbed that pan and put most of the corn on Suzi's plate. Ralphie said, "I got that corn for my son . . . that's all he'll eat." Dad growled, "That's too damn bad." Alice's kids didn't even stand a chance. Dad wouldn't even look at em. So she got the picture pretty quick. Ann persisted though. She was thrilled when dad actually got to where he'd hold the boys on his lap once in awhile when he was doin' the cross word puzzle. But that was about it. One time when her kids got a little older they drug Suzi's tricycle outta the basement. They were ridin' it around . . . crashin' into things. Dad come in drunk and took it away from em. "Suzi'll want this some day," he growled. Those boys were so hurt . . . they cried and cried. The next day, dad came in with 2 little red bikes he'd got at the hardware store. "Here," he said. "Now you leave Suzi's alone." Ann beamed. She was so happy to see dad takin' an interest in her kids.

"Unfit Mother"

When dad was sober, he'd just say that I wasn't "old enough yet" . . . to take my daughter. He'd say she was better off right where she was . . . there with them. I know he loved Suzi. He liked to brag at the tavern about how much she ate. Sometimes he'd get in drunk and he'd pick her up and waltz her around the house. He'd scrounge around for some crap to feed her and then he'd open him a beer and take a gulp. He'd sit down on the couch, bounce her on his knee and then look at me real mean and growl, "Don't git any big ideas . . . you ain't ever gittin' this baby." Then he'd slam the beer can down on the coffee table. I endured that bullshit for years.

But finally, when she was 12, I just knew that the half dozen donuts he fed her for breakfast and the half dozen hot dogs he fed her for dinner was no good . . . was nothin' to go on about to anybody. I decided then to just take Suzi. I drove up there, marched in and said, "I'm takin' *my* daughter." I didn't know what he'd do . . . hit me . . . shoot me . . . call the cops. He just stood there, starin' at me, smokin' a cigarette. He didn't do anything . . . he caved in like a wet card board box. I quickly packed her little blue suitcase and we got in the truck. He came out on the porch. Suzi waved to him. I took off and drove 800 miles. I only stopped for gas.

Advanced Degree

One day I got a wild hair and decided to go to Law School and by god . . . I got in. I loved studyin' those big old books. But I knew I wasn't gonna ever amount to anything in that profession. I didn't care about the law that much. I just wanted an achievement so dad would like me. I went home after my first year. Dad come in from work with a 12 pack. I tried to tell him about torts and contracts and criminal procedure. He didn't even seem interested. He just kept talkin' about the factory. He kept wantin' to tell me how fast some new girl could put envelopes in a box. "Boy, she's a hell of a packer," he'd say, "I can hardly keep up with her." I couldn't believe it. Finally I said, "Dad, I don't even know that envelope packin' fool . . . why do you think I want to hear about her?" He looked at me and said, "Everybody's jealous of her . . . she's showin' em all up . . . she's showin' em how it should be done." That was it for me. I got up from the table. I grabbed my beer and said, "Dad why don't you ask that dumb bitch if SHE'S on the god damn dean's list." I walked outta the kitchen and I left the next day. I went back and finished up my studies and graduated. But dad never did seem to care. In fact I don't believe he gave a shit one way or the other that I'd become a Doctor of Jurisprudence.

Dad's Big Girl

Suzi was home once when Alice came down with her brood. They were always alittle afraid of Suzi because as far as dad was concerned, his favorite granddaughter could do no wrong. Suzi was the princess around that place. It made Alice so mad. She was fit to be tied that dad had never really liked her or her kids much. She let her kids destroy all the thread in mom's little sewing basket once. "Leave dat alone . . . leave dat alone," mom yelled. They didn't listen to mom. They just threw it around, pulled it off the spools and tangled it all up as Alice watched smiling. Later Suzi went to sew on a button and she went wild when she saw that mess. She cursed Alice, she pushed her around, said she was gonna throw her through the wall, said she was gonna kill her kids. Alice tried to stand up for herself but what could she really do . . . dad was just sittin' there at the table watchin' Suzi go nuts and he didn't do anything to stop her. Alice stood there and kept saying "I don't have to leave . . . this is MY father's house and he 'sired' me." Suzi called her a "frigging farm animal." By now, Alice's kids were trembling and crying. Finally Alice grabbed her purse and out they went. She was definitely not that important to dad. At the end he forgot her name and just referred to her as "His Worker."

"Pretty in Pink"

You can't even have your own favorite color around Alice. She's too insecure to let you like royal blue or emerald green. She just can't let it rest and accept that you don't like pastels. She refuses to believe that you don't endorse her choices by makin' them your own. She takes it so personal. Once she got so upset. She screamed and hollered like a maniac, "What's wrong with peach . . . or mint or beige . . . women should wear soft delicate colors . . . men like colors like that on women . . . feminine colors . . . like this," she said. She stood up. I looked at my sister . . . all 200 pounds of her in pale yellow. I said, "I see what you mean." Then I put on my scarlet red sweater and went outside.

"Well If It's Too Much Mom . . . Just Don't Eat It All"

Once mom came to visit me. She was so awful and demanding. She expected to be waited on hand and foot. And nothing I did was good enough or quite right. "Ver ees my juice, Landa?" "Vat about dee donut?" "Dat kafee ees too hot!" "Ees dat all dee cereal I get?" "Can't you at least cut up dee banana?" And there was never a word of appreciation. Never a compliment. One time I screamed at her, "Mom, I get up every fuckin' day and instead of throwin' you in the street, I put an apron on and make you a nice breakfast. This morning all you need to say to me is THANKS . . . you got that?" I slammed her plate down in front of her. She sat there lookin' at the food and then she said, "Vel, ok Landa . . . I tank you very much but you know I don't like dee beeg Schredded Wheat . . . I like dee schpoon size."

"I Just Luff
Nice Tings to Ver"

I worked on mom's jackets today. The ones she got at Kmart on sale. I hemmed the sleeves. She modeled them for me. She loves bein' a size 4 Petite, like some old scrawny rich woman. But mom didn't starve down on tiny servings of elegant cuisine . . . she just forgot to eat 'cause she's nuts. She keeps askin' me if I hat done my dentures yet? And I keep saying, "No mom, I ain't got dentures . . . my teeth are real." "Oh," she says, "Der so nice und schtraight . . . just like dentures." I turn back to my notebook. She starts asking me, "Vy do you haf to vaste so much time vid all dat writing?" I look up. She's put on the pink coat AGAIN and is twirling around. I look back at the hateful meanness I've scrawled on the paper and then I say, "Mom, I'm writin' a story . . . a beautiful story about YOU." She smiles real big at that and says, "Vel vy jist a schtory Landa, you coult write a whole buch about me." I look at her and say, "Well a *book* about you, huh, that wouldn't be a waste of time now would it mom?" "Oh no," she exclaims, "I'm a wery interesting person." She's got on the blue coat now and is spinning madly around the room.

"She Likes Soup"

It's impossible to tell the time even though there are 6 clocks in this place. Not a single one is accurate. The cheap plastic one in the "green room" has birds on it and emits a kind of chirping noise, not on the hour, but when ever it wants to. She loves it. Calls it her coo-coo. She makes sure it's kept wound. It's amazing what the meals have deteriorated to. How did it get worse than it was? Her potato salad brought me to tears. It used to be ok. She would actually use mayonaise and add mustard and spices and vinegar and sugar and chopped up eggs and pickle relish with onions. Now it's pulp cooked taters and boiled eggs with a bottle of salad dressing dumped on top. She hardly drained the potatoes so it's an awful watery goober. The macaroni and cheese is store bought individual servings in small aluminum pie pans. She heats them up in the oven which she forgets to turn off. She opens a package of hot dogs and a can of kraut. There's white bread and margarine in a tub. She's got it all out on the table. The bird clock squawks 10 times and we pull out our chairs. I fill up my paper plate and I tell her it looks delicious. Mom beams proudly. I sit there with her and I eat that slop . . . I actually EAT THAT SLOP.

"Ain't Nothin' Wrong with You"

Once Ann was out some where with Alice and Phillip and she started gettin' sick. Her head started hurtin' so bad. But Alice refused to take her home. It was a beautiful summer afternoon and she didn't want her plans messed up. She said, "You don't have a headache. I know. Your eyes are brown. Phillip's eyes are blue and everyone knows blue eyes are way more sensitive than brown. If Phillip doesn't have a headache . . . there's no way you can . . . you liar."

"She's Just Peddlin' Dope Up There"

In my family no one gave you credit for doin' anything. You couldn't get a compliment to save your life. If you had an achievement they didn't want to hear about it. But I moved to N.Y.C. and they got curious. They really couldn't pretend to be too disinterested after that. One time I was home, Alice sat there squirmin'. She really didn't want to listen but she sure couldn't get up. I went on and on about my store. I told her all about my customers. How I was makin' clothes for movies and T.V. shows. How I was a success. How I was meetin' celebrities and rich people. How I was written up in magazines. Alice wasn't smilin'. She just glared at me. She narrowed her eyes and went, "Hmmmm." Then she growled, "Have you ever been audited, Linda?"

Hell on a
House Boat

One summer we were all down in southern Illinois and Ralphie went out to Kincaid Lake and rented a boat. It was a pretty big deal for us . . . a family get together. Mom pranced aboard in short shorts. Dad was only worried about havin' enough beer. Alice was too big to even have a swimmin' suit now. Ann showed up with Rainbow who couldn't keep his hands off of her. The fightin' started before Ralphie even pulled away from the dock. Mom snappin' at Alice. Alice snarlin' back. I called her a monster. She called me a loser and a drunk and she said she knew why my husband was the way he was. "Dope," she yelled. "He's a dope fiend." It was just one insult after another. Ralphie tried to keep it light. He decided to teach mom to steer the boat. "Mom cain't drive a boat," Alice yelled. "Mom cain't do anything." Mom sat there hangin' onto the wheel with both hands as we chugged along. She had no idea what she was doin'. She wouldn't even change direction when we veered toward shore. "Go right . . . go right," I yelled. "Turn it . . . turn it," Ralphie said. He grabbed the wheel just in time and mom proceeded to act like she hadn't almost crashed us into the bank. "See?" Alice screamed. "See?" Mom got up and opened her another beer. Alice really looked down on us. She counted the empty cans and rolled her eyes and hurrumphed. She wouldn't shut up about how "bad" we were and how "good" she was . . . the best one in the family 'cause she abstained from alcoholic liquor. Damn, I drank so much that day. I really did. I drank so much, that unfortunately, I only have a vague recollection of tryin' to throw that teetotaling bitch over board.

"I'll Get Me a Second Opinion, Thank You"

I was shocked when Alice just up and called me one day. Some superficial pleasantries exchanged and then she quickly tried to get to the point . . . her tone turned urgent . . . somber. There was something she just had to tell me. Well, I start talkin' a mile a minute, saying anything . . . upbeat . . . positive . . . incoherant, just rambling because she's waiting for her chance . . . waiting to pounce with her premonition that just had to be delivered right now 'cause she "cared about me." I wasn't interested. I knew better. I try to keep talking but finally she screams, "You have to get to a hospital *now* . . . promise me you'll go *now* . . . go as fast as you can." I try at first to drown her out . . . but she's got some mean words: "tumor, malignancy, cancer, sarcoma," and they just drop kick my happy crap and I'm shocked and speechless. And Jesus, here she comes again with stuff like: "chemo, radiation therapy, and bone marrow transplant." She's agitated . . . eager. And then she proceeds with a detailed description of the DREAM she had had about me the night before. "IT was *so real*," she said enthusiastically. And then there's more medical terminology. She really enunciates the words . . . pronounces them perfectly. And I hear statements of statistical survival rates. She's really acting like a doctor with a real diagnosis, holding up a real X ray to some real patient. "It was a black mass . . . grade 4." She's proving a point . . . dropping a death sentence . . . my death sentence . . . so coldly . . . out of the blue and I'm hating her. Finally she pauses . . . there's silence . . . and then she barks, "Well . . . aren't you even going to thank me?" Surprisingly somehow, I'm able to speak and I say "Alice, FUCK YOU and your bed side manner." She slams the phone down.

Any Time's the
Right Time

I had so many fights with Ralphie about how he took mom's money for anything and everything he did for her. He "odd jobbed" her outta so much cash. I hated the way he was a grown man suckin' off that old lady. He'd say, "Well . . . she NEVER gave me nothin'." It was despicable. I'd say, "Dad did for gramma and he never charged her . . . in fact, dad gave gramma money . . . every week . . . remember?" Ralphie never commented on that. He liked to say, "My time's valuable," and I'd say, "No it isn't . . . you fuckin' bastard." I couldn't make him see how pathetic it was . . . how bad he looked. Maybe he knew . . . maybe he didn't care. Ralphie was 40 something years old. To me he was robbin' mom . . . to him he was just gettin' what he had comin'. Better late than never.

He Was Gonna
Major in Philosophy

After Ralphie's kids got pretty much grown he decided to go to college. He was a 45 year old man runnin' around campus with a book bag he'd made himself from choppin' the legs off a pair of jeans and then sewin' a seam. He was proud of that thing. He slung it over his shoulder and marched into his freshman classes. He got through a couple of semesters with pretty good grades. Then his scholarship money and benefits got cut and he was gonna have to quit. This was a perfect opportunity to bad mouth the government even though he was already tired of the college deal. He said how could he make it on what they were gonna give him. He said he wouldn't even be able to eat on that. He said, "They shouldn't fuck with the G.I. bill . . . that's no way to treat soldiers." Then he said some stuff about how he'd served his country in the military and now they were kickin' him in the ass. He was so up set. He was startin' to lie. He kept sayin' "I'm a Vietnam Vet . . . I'm a Vietnam Vet." Finally I said, "What the hell are you talkin' about Ralphie . . . you ain't a Vietnam Vet." He looked up and sort of came to his senses. Then he said, "Well . . . I almost was . . . they tried to get me."

"They Shit on ME"

I don't believe Ralphie's paid any taxes for the last 15 years. He just says he ain't got the money to pay taxes. He says he works too damn hard for the little bit he gets. He says he ain't about to give any of it to the government. He hates the government. He says the government should be ashamed to come after people like him . . . people below the poverty line. He says he ain't even got the money to get his teeth fixed. He says there's no way he's gonna give up food for the god damn government. He said in the beginning he paid. He said he didn't mind back then. But when he got down on his luck and a little behind they went in and cleaned out his bank account. Took all 300 dollars he had in there. He said he wrote em a letter: Dear IRS, Please cut me some slack. I'll pay what I owe soon. He signed it Sincerely yours! Ralphie said, "Those bastards didn't even write me back . . . they probably didn't even read my letter . . . they just took all my money . . . they're the criminals . . . not me." So now Ralphie just odd jobs it around town for cash. He can't own anything except his tools. He never lies about how much he makes. If he earns $8,000 one year that's what he puts down. He fills out the form. Not the E-Z short form but all the complicated pages he can get his hands on at the post office or send off for. He's got an income tax return thick enough for a million dollar company. He likes to make it complicated. He figures out just exactly what they say he owes and then he sends all that stuff off with out a penny. He likes to imagine what they think when they open up the package and they don't get anything but paper work. "What are they gonna do to me?" he laughs. "Put me in jail 'cause I'm a pauper?" He says, "I'm better than them people . . . at least I'm honest . . . they're liars and thieves . . . they STOLED my money . . . those bastards owe me an apology . . . I'm a U.S. Citizen."

Good Work If
You Can Get It

The Shawnee Forest put out a call for part time workers. They needed acorns gathered so they could reseed a tract of oak trees that wasn't doin' well. Ralphie signed on. He was between things and figured he could do somethin' good for the woods and maybe earn alittle money. And when I say "maybe" . . . I mean maybe. The whole time he was out there crawlin' around on his hands and knees he was worried . . . worried that if the IRS called up the Forest Service or vice versa that'd be it for him. He wouldn't make out on that deal at all. Finally after 3 weeks of back breakin' work, the project was over. Everybody showed up on pay day. Even the lazy trash who'd give out after collectin' just afew bushels. A guy handed out checks. Finally Ralphie's name was called. He actually got one. He stood there lookin' at it. "See what I mean about the government," he said. "They don't know what they're doin' . . . those stupid bastards . . . they paid me."

"It Goes for
$50 a Pound"

Ralphie collected ginseng to offset his income. He found it out in the woods and sold it to man who came through town once a month. He got paid in cash and that worked out good for him. He didn't want to worry about any kind of tax repercussions. He got so good at finding ginseng. We'd be lookin' somewhere way out in the Shawnee Forest . . . he'd stop and point . . . he could spot a plant from a mile away. Sometimes he wouldn't even pull it up. "Too little," he'd say and we'd walk on. He'd get that one next year. He really knew where to look . . . "north side of a hill . . . nice and shady." He knew all about ginseng! The history of it. How it had been used for thousands of years by lots of cultures. He also became an expert on all the things ginseng can do for you. "It'll cure anything," he'd say. He could really extoll its virtues. He talked about how people used it for everything . . . "diabetus," lethargy and cancer. "It's a proven remedy. It ain't snake oil . . . ginseng works." I looked at him and said, "Ralphie does it work for you?" He sort of laughed and said, "I never tried it . . . I ain't about to try that stuff."

"You Got Any Money . . . He Needs Him a New Transmission"

Well, he's special, he's the last to carry on the St. John name. So whatever my nephew wanted that my brother could get for him, he got. And the boy was never called upon to do anything . . . not a single chore. All work fell on Ralph's daughter, Wendy. "But he was alot younger than her back then." "No he wasn't," I yell. "He wasn't any younger than her back then than he is now." And he would only eat certain things and Jesus, the suppositories that went up his special ass because frozen chocolate donuts were his favorite food. He was 5 years old jumpin' up and down, "I wanna 'pository . . . wanna 'pository." One year he even got an electric train, it was sold 2 weeks later to pay the rent. He got the best room . . . near the heat. He beat on the little girl and never got in trouble. Wendy the slave did all the work. Cooked . . . cleaned . . . washed. At supper, a regular meal for the family and a special separate meal for him: A) a H-burger w/tater chips or B) a H-dog w/corn doodles. NO SUBSTITUTIONS. She finally just left at 18, came to N.Y. Who cooked for the constipated prince on a pillow then? Not his mother who always plopped it on the couch and whined for her cup of coffee. When things fell apart up here, Wendy went to Texas and tried to help him out. He drove his rattletrap down there and got on at the restaurant . . . lasted 2 weeks and then mid-shift he threw his rag down and "I ain't worshin' another plate." He made it back to my brother's in 12 hours. He sleeps . . . eats . . . sleeps . . . eats. He's 28 years old. He leaves notes for Ralphie . . . grocery notes. He drinks whole bottles of cooking wine, stalks around out in the woods and *won't* help my brother on the roofin' jobs. He just screams and yells and threatens to kill him. Especially if Ralphie makes too much noise with his fork when he's eatin' or if he sits cross legged and his flip flop slaps the bottom of his foot too loud. And if Ralphie belches . . . the boy goes crazy. He starts hollering at my brother. "Say it . . . say it . . . say: 'Excuse me, excuse me, excuse me,' . . . say it . . . say it or I'll KILL YOU," he screams, "say it 3 TIMES."

Killed by Kindness

I knew all that half assed stuff Ralphie did for his son was bullshit. That wasn't for the son. That was for Ralphie himself. That stupid absurd effort to give him everything and treat him special. And Ralphie put so much time and energy on the "kindness." It was like a project. Ralphie was just tryin' to show dad up . . . prove him wrong . . . make up for all the meanness. The kid knew he was a pawn. It was obvious. My brother was like a drowning man tryin' to float some where on his son.

"How Could He
Be My Relative?"

One fall Ralphie wrangled a job workin' on a guy's cabin. He hadn't seen mom in years and I had a chance to take her up there. It was a 4 hour drive. Ralphie didn't smile when he saw us. Mom hugged him but he kept his arms to his side. He just stood there stiff. Little Ralphie was there too but he was so fat mom didn't know who he was. Mom thought he was just some guy helpin' Ralphie. We hung around and talked alittle and then they had to get to work. Me and mom went to look for a motel. There was room in the cabin but Ralphie hadn't asked us to stay. We drove around but couldn't find a place that would take us and the dog. Finally I stopped at a camp site and a man said he'd rent me a pop-up camper but I'd need my own sleeping bags. I told Ralphie we didn't have sleeping bags. I said, "We'd need some covers and pillows." All he could say was, "Well . . . why don't you jist make it a day trip . . . jist make it a day trip." It was almost dark now and gettin' cold. Me and mom were tired. We weren't gonna be able to "jist make it a day trip." I stood there lookin' at Ralphie . . . that useless prick. He didn't give a shit about me and mom. His answer to the dilemma was for me to just start drivin'. I couldn't believe it . . . but then again, of course I could. Finally little Ralphie got up and started rounding up quilts and bed spreads and covers. He made a big pile by the door and said, "You can use these . . . we don't need em." Me and mom took that stuff and went back to the camp site. We bundled up and managed to stay warm. The next morning we dropped the covers off and just left. Mom said, "Ralph don't look goot Landa . . . I hardly recognized him." "Yeah," I said, "He's a god damn stranger . . . always has been."

Three Ralphs
on a Couch

Once I took a picture of dad, Ralphie and little Ralphie. It was one of the few times my brother and nephew came up to visit after dad got sick. They just sat there so uncomfortable . . . lookin' straight ahead. Nobody had their arm around the other. Nobody smiled. The minute I clicked the camera they got up and got away from each other.

A Fool Proof
System

After the radiation treatments he was the best he was since the operation and he really started focusing on the lotto. He knew he probably wasn't goin' back to work so he decided to come up with a system to hit it big. He got a piece of card board and taped a large sheet of unlined white paper on it. Then he proceeded to devise an elaborate chart. He drew all kinds of lines and arrows. He created categories. He labeled sections. He made diagrams. He put down some numbers and letters and then got out colored pencils to shade certain areas like a graph. It was totally convoluted and incomprehensible. He propped it up on the table and studied it. He referred to it as he wrote combinations on a separate piece of paper. He tried to explain it to me. "See," he said. "Now the 24 works for 3 and the 36, 37 and 39 don't work for one but could and the 12 goes for ought . . ." I just said, "Well . . . ok dad . . . it looks good to me."

Death and Taxes

Dad always did his own taxes. Nothin' hard about that for him. But after his operation he had so much trouble. He really tried to add up some numbers and fill out the form. But he just didn't know what was goin' on now. There was alot more to it than ought plus ought equals ought. He realized that and he was so upset. He said, "By god . . . them tax people better not come after me . . . they cain't arrest me . . . I ain't even *got* a brain anymore."

Lotto Stubs

It's mostly sittin' at the kitchen table now. Sittin' and smokin' and rubbin' his head. He's still weak. His scalp must itch and hurt. He showed me some lotto tickets and proclaimed, "This is it!" They were 3 weeks old. It's so dark in here—the curtains are all drawn, closed tight. They aren't even hemmed, just whacked off so they won't drag the floor. The edge is cut jagged, uneven all the way across. The threads dangle down. They used to be beige (she just loves beige), now they're a vulgar piss yellow. The cigarette smoke, it's coated everything with a hideous film, an awful layer of gummy crap. You can scratch it off the rocking chair with your fingernail. Black gunk from thousands and thousands of burning cigarettes. He just stares, holding the cig—he watches the smoke go up as it begins the process of coating the room. He's looking at the lotto stubs, intently staring, carefully rescrutinizing them and rubbing his head and grunting occasionally and saying "hmmmm . . ." and puffing on the cigarette and squinting his eyes from the swirling smoke and then saying "Hells bells . . . god damn it to hell."

It's hard for me to breathe. My face aches. I look at him. "Get any winners dad?" He looks up and sort of laughs. "Naw . . . noo . . . never have . . . bastards."

Prayer Session

For awhile there was some talk about "re-operating." Goin' in and cuttin' out what had grown back. Dad didn't want that. He didn't want anyone to mess around with his head anymore. So they just increased the medication and then let him come home. This time he was better for only a short while. He was able to ride his bike alittle at first. He could even make it out to the Bi-rite and come back with some groceries. He was proud of that. He started talkin' again about all the things he wanted to do around this place and then followed each pronouncement with the phrase, "If I git to feelin' better . . . if I git to feelin' better." We prayed up stairs in our rooms and when dad didn't get to feelin' better . . . we cursed god . . . called him a no good non-existent bastard. We turned our misery on each other. We fought and cried and carried on. We blamed one another for everything including the cancer that was chewin' up dad. We wanted us a miracle so bad . . . we had one comin' . . . we had *never* asked for anything. God let us down completely. It was a farce . . . hands together . . . head bowed . . . beggin' like that.

Silent Stare

My niece was just 11 years old, a little girl. She hadn't been around them much. But she was happy to come on the "family" outing with me and mom and dad. She could tell that something was really wrong with dad. "Why, grampa can't hardly walk," she said. Me and her slept on one double bed, mom and dad on the other. I dreaded waking up in that motel room to that whole day ahead of us. Nothin' to do but wait for Saturday night. He wouldn't eat anything and he couldn't be left alone—the matches—the cigarettes. We went to Hardees. They both sat there smoking all day long. Mom bitched and hollered and lit cigs for both of em. When we got back, Becky sat on the bed, patiently, quietly. I sat with her and looked out the open door of our room to the hills and fields of my childhood. Back here again because even dogs go home to die. I looked at mom and dad connected now only by the striking of matches, the lighting of cigarettes, the swirling of smoke. I saw mom glance up and survey the room. Her eyes narrowed on Becky. She turned to me and angrily yelled, "Vy ees dat leedle girl looking at me like dat?" "Mom," I screamed, "dat leedle girl is your granddaughter, you fucking moron."

Down to Zero

Dad was back to lining up old lotto stubs and lookin' at the cross word puzzle he couldn't fill in and the newspaper he couldn't read. The same old routine. He drank coffee and ice water and lit cigarette after cigarette . . . just sittin' there. He swallowed the pills mom laid out for him and he ate the slop that she brought in on a tray. But one day he couldn't ride the bicycle anymore. He was out in the yard fixin' to get on it and he nearly fell over. The bike was layin' in the grass and he was standin' there. Mom ran out screamin', "Dat bike ees wery dengerous Landa . . . dat bike ees wery dengerous." She picked it up and pushed it back behind the garage. He couldn't do anything but watch her go. Then he turned to me and whispered, "I tried . . . I tried." I took his arm and said, "I know dad . . . I know." I helped him back up the porch . . . back to the kitchen table . . . back to the few things he would still have for awhile longer.

Nicotine Fit

This time when he goes in things are pretty bad. They give him steroids again to shrink the swelling. He responds a little bit . . . enough to need a smoke. He can't hardly strike a match anymore. "Shit," he says. Just tryin' and fumblin' and cussin' with matches goin' everywhere . . . droppin' some burning ones on the floor but unable to light the cig between his lips. "God damn it to hell."

This is the 1st time the nurses have taken his cigarettes away from him. He almost set his bed afire and will not be allowed to smoke unattended.

Sitting now in the lounge, still unable to coordinate the match, the flame and the cigarette but cravin' that nicotine and needin' it in his blood stream, my father turns to me and whispers, "Could I have one please?" I just look at him . . . I don't know what to think . . . I am worried . . . this mean and rough man has NEVER said please before.

Fire Fighter

Mom said he kept asking, "Where is she . . . where is she?" I was coming. I wasn't going to let him down. We stayed at the Gateway Inn, only afew miles from the reunion grounds. Saturday night would be the big night. If any body was going to be there who knew him, it would be then. Any old army buddies, school mates, poker playin'–beer drinkin' pals. Somebody he could speak to after all these years—connect with in some way. That's all he wanted. He sat at the little motel table with her across from him. They had their "set-ups" out. Cigarettes, lighters and matches . . . just in case. He didn't move the whole day, just sittin', waitin' and smokin'. Droppin' lit cigarettes on himself and the chair. "Rolf, you are goink to brurn des place up," she kept screaming at him. "No . . . not me . . ." he would mumble. She kept getting up and pawing at the ashes on his pants and counting burn holes in the upholstry of the chair. Sometimes he'd try to light the filter end and when he couldn't get any draw, he'd growl "fuck it" and flip the cigarette anywhere. "Look dat carpet ees schmouldering now," she said pointing at the floor. She started stompin'. "Landa," she screamed at me. "You vatch him now." She quickly grabbed a big plastic take-out cup, ran to the bathroom and filled it up. She charged back in and slammed it down right in the middle of the table, water spilling everywhere. "I might haf to trow dis on him," she announced as she sat back down and picked up her cig.

Maybe Somebody
Will Say, "Hi, Ralph"

Ann had said to throw a wheel chair in the back of the truck, just in case. He'd never go for that. It'd hurt him too much for people to see him unable to walk and sure enough when he saw the chair, he just shook his head and said, "Uh uh . . . not me." I help him to the curb and we get in the car and start off. The rain lets up that evening as we finally pull into the outskirts of Stonefort. I can see the lights of the carnival under the trees. The place is crowded so we have to park way across the hard road in the grass. I go around and open dad's door. He can barely swing his legs and scoot off the seat. He just stands there. He can't walk. She gets out and starts bitchin' and yellin'. "Des man ees seek. Vy did you haf to make him come to dis place? Vee haf to go." I want to punch my mom in the face . . . but my concern is dad coming home to die. He's seized up somehow in his brain and he just can't put one foot in front of the other. I get the wheel chair out. "No . . . not me," he starts mumbling. He's trying so hard to make his feet move. Nothing is happening. I push the chair up to him. "Please daddy . . . sit down." Finally he drops himself into the seat and I try to push him. But I can't move the wheel chair, it's bogging down in the soggy unmowed grass. It won't go. *It won't fucking go.* She keeps screaming at me and I can't move the chair. "No . . . not me," he says. We are sinking down in the muddy water and the grass is grabbin' the wheels. I try to push again. I don't want to tip him over. "You are keeling dis man," she yells. "You are keeling dis man." "Son of a bitch," I scream. "Just please god, let me get it *started* . . . then I can roll it and get him over there so he can at least sit and maybe somebody will come by and say 'Hi Ralph.' That's all he wants," I cry out. People are staring at us now. "Ve haf to go, ve haf to go, Landa," she *yells* and *yells* and *yells*. Finally, I just grab the handles of the wheel chair and scream *"God damn it to Hell,"* and I literally pick the thing up . . . I hold it out in front of me like a T.V. tray and son of a bitch, I *carry* dad toward the bright lights and wild music.

Enjoyin' the Show

I get him a coffee with powdered creamer in a Styrofoam cup and he stands one hand on his hip, legs locked, feet planted. His eyes dart around from person to person, to anyone he might know, who might know him. Afew old men stop to talk and he nods and mutters incoherent things like "we'll get em, gonna get em, win lose or draw." But the square dancing starts up and eyes turn to swirling dresses and petticoats goin' round and round and the old men move on. Dad is getting tired anyway. She gives him a smoke and he looks at me and then just sits down in the wheel chair. Up on the stage a geezer spins off in a solo routine . . . like a beer bellied scare crow on a string—perfectly immobile from the waist up but going crazy from the waist down—working his legs like a puppet on dope trying to dig through the floor boards with his big white plastic shoes. Dad sits there smokin'—watchin'. Then she starts to yell at me about "dat noise und lout music" and "how vee need to get because he ees a wery seek man." I just yell at her, "He's not *sick*, you idiot, he's dyin'. "

"It Always Backed Up"

Somehow he got up and got in there by himself. He's leaning over . . . one hand on the sink . . . one on the wall. He's growlin . . . groanin'. He tries the handle again . . . he jiggles it . . . nothin' happens. He says, "Hells bells." He almost loses his balance. The water and mess rise higher in the bowl. Mom charges in screamin' . . . she pushes him aside. She grabs the plunger and works the toilet. She grabs the mop and yells, "Dat's not my fault . . . I hat vanted to geet dat damn tawlet feexed for years." I help him into the bed room. He can barely walk. I can see his skinny legs through his pajamas when we go past the lamp on the dresser. He used to be strong and stout. I saw the old army picture of him runnin' . . . winnin' that race. He was so far ahead of everybody. Best of a 1,000 men. Now he sits on the edge of the bed hardly able to make it to the bathroom. She walks through yellin' and bitchin' about "everyting een dis dump ees falling apart und dat's not right to haf to lif dis vay." He just lays down and doesn't even tell her to go to hell.

Things Change . . .
Swamps Are Drained

I drove dad everywhere lookin' for that stand of cane that grew in the bottom lands of Saline County. Not many people knew about that strange swampy area hidden in the Shawnee Forest. When we were little, he'd take us there every spring to get our fishin' poles. We'd cut a couple dozen 15 footers, tie em up and put em in the car . . . one end of the bundle resting on the floor board, the other end sticking out the back window. Then dad would take off . . . our beat up '51 Chevy bumpin' down that country road. We'd turn around and look out and pretend we were in some far away place. It could have even been China. He'd wind around forever and finally come out in southern Illinois some where on the highway. We never really knew where we were for sure but dad did. And then there'd be Saturday afternoons at Crab Orchard Lake and stringers full of fish staked up to the bank. We were livin' off the fat of the land. Dad really liked that and now that he was sick he wanted to see that cane again. I couldn't remember anything and neither could he . . . at this point. I stopped and asked afew old people . . . "We're lookin' for the cane." "The what?" they'd say. Dad could only nod and mumble. Everywhere we went it wasn't there. He wanted to see that memory so bad and I just couldn't find it. By night fall I felt like I was goin' in circles. I looked over at dad and said, "That sure was some fine eatin' we caught with them cane poles. Remember how we fought one another over that fish you fried up . . . Remember them salted tails . . . they were better than potato chips." He smiled and grunted but he wasn't about to give up. He just kept pointin' straight ahead toward the dark dirt road we were goin' down.

Spit Bath

When he felt like he was on fire . . . mom sponged him down. He couldn't wash himself at that point or do anything to relieve his suffering. She'd put the cool water on him and jabber and talk nuts. She still liked to say, "We're gonna beat dis ting."

He weighed 120 pounds. He sat there naked on the toilet. She'd dip the rag in the sink and rub his back and shoulders. She'd rub it across his forehead. "Don't vorry babe," she'd tell him. She'd keep sayin' he'd be better soon . . . that everything would be ok. All she did was lie. She put his house coat on him and helped him outta the bathroom. She was really on one of her positive kicks and he'd had enough of her crap. He just looked at her and growled, "You jist make sure they put me 6 feet under the ground."

The Tyrant
Wears Diapers

He'd always said he was "gonna die at home . . . by god." He made mom promise that. But it reached a point where mom couldn't take care of him anymore. She just wasn't able. So one day when Alice was there, they packed afew of his clothes and took him up to Sunny Acres. When they got in the place he realized where he was and what was happenin'. Alice said he got so mad. She said, "He turned around and tried to lunge for mom." She said he looked at mom like he wanted to kill her. But mom wasn't afraid. He wasn't the boss anymore. He wasn't makin' the decisions. Alice said it was sad how when the two big orderlies came up, he didn't act belligerent to them . . . he just went down the hall to his new room.

Final Word

As dad got closer to the end, he kept losin' more and more of his words. The cancer was really eatin' them up now . . . , one right after the other. Eventually he was down to just a few words and grunts. Alice and mom would go visit him and no matter what they said, his answer would be the same: "Hells bells," "Cigarette," "Uh uh," or "Augh," etc. Lots of times he wouldn't say anything at all . . . just lay there starin' at the ceiling. By November, he'd pretty well quit eatin'. They tried to feed him Thanksgiving dinner and they said it was like tryin' to feed a baby that hadn't learned to swallow. Come December, dad couldn't sit up without bein' strapped to his chair. I don't believe he was speakin' at all by then. Alice and mom said they went up there on his birthday and found him in the hall. Someone had left him there, starin' out the window. He didn't seem to know who they were. On the 22nd, the nursing home called. A lady said, "He don't seem too good today." Alice hurried right over there. The lobby was decorated for Christmas. There were colorful paper cut outs everywhere and they'd put up a pretty tree with bright lights. Grade school kids were singing "Come All Ye Faithful." Dad was in his room sittin' in his wheel chair. "Daddy daddy," Alice exclaimed, "Let me push you down the hall so you can hear the Christmas Carols," And dad who didn't seem to understand a thing and who hadn't even spoken a word in weeks, threw his head back, opened his mouth and growled real loud, "NO!" That was the last word that he ever spoke. Dad died the next day.

"When I Die, the Whole Town Will Show Up for My Funeral"

They said nobody much came. Mom didn't have a service for him at home so that shut the locals out up there. She didn't know how to arrange anything like that. And most of the people down home in Stonefort were gone or dead themselves. A few old timers did show up at the funeral home. Ralphie said maybe 15 people. He said it was nice.

Father and Son

I didn't want to see my dad put in the ground. I didn't go to the funeral. But Ralphie did. He showed up with a beat-up old guitar that he'd got at some junk store. Alice said he did "500 Miles," "She'll Be Comin' Round the Mountain" and "Little Brown Church in the Dell." She said he just sang his heart out and cried. I know the tears were mostly for himself. The songs at least were ones he thought dad might like. Alice said it was too much to take. She said he was so off key and he couldn't even play that guitar. Shit . . . I know it must have been a spectacle how he beat on that thing and wailed and moaned from the bottom of his heart 'cause he was a grown man now . . . a grown man whose chances for a dad were over.

Drunk Drivin'

When he was roarin' down the road drunk, one eye closed so he wouldn't see double, cussin' at the radio—bottom of the 8th—Cardinals losin'. Lightin' up a cig . . . fightin' the wind . . . both hands bent around the match, the Chevy rockin', bouncin' around . . . the flame gone out . . . strike another match . . . "god damn it to hell" . . . and another . . . "god damn it to hell" . . . smoke finally swirling from the cig . . . He grabs the wheel, pullin' the car off the shoulder . . . just in time . . . jerkin' across the yellow line . . . a truck driver honkin', raisin' his fist, shakin' it at us.

"You missed him by an inch," I cry out looking at dad.

"Inch is as good as a mile," he laughs. "Inch is as good as a mile."

Acknowledgments

To the following people who, each in their own way, helped to make this book a reality. Thank you all for your support and encouragement. Becky Kurson, Marjorie Braman, Laurie Rippon, Jennifer Baumgardner, Amy Ray, Steve Earle, Laurie Seeman, Judi Farkas, Phyllis Kind, Giancarlo Esposito, Joy McManigal, Betty Carol Sellen, Louisa Chase, Margaret Bodell, Carlos Sanches, Elenor and Tom Kovachevich, Elsa and Bill Longhauser, Cecelia and Michael Dan, Kevin Conley, Owen Phillips, Chris Curry, Stuart Servetar, Dick Cavett, Carrie Nye, Bob Roth, Mieke van Hoek, Meredith Monk, Stefan Springman, Danny Davis, John and Gina Phelan, Barbara Stratton, Ron Hammond, Chris Giglio, Gloria Jacobs, Carl Glassman, April Koral, Eve Claxton, Donna Ferrato, Shelly Taylor, Joe Cook, Judy Mae Cornett, Keith Blue, Ellen Kuras, David Utz, Bond Koga, Alan Rapp, Jane Koprucki, Joan and William Huffman, Dianne and Danny Vapnek, Hiroko Tanaka, Ed and Pat Martz, Ethel Greaney, Ken Kurson, Staci Strauss, Anna and Orest Szczesniuk, Millie and Howie Bodell, Ilene and Lester Bliwise, Betsy Haddad, D. James Smith, Brian Booms, Margaret and Jorge Ambrosoni, Diana Kunkel, Colette Kunkel, Yictove, Lester Bridges, Niels Koizumi, Mark and Karen Rubinstein, Christopher Johnsen, David McDonagh, Doug Bridgeman, Matthew Bishop, Robert and Ana Costello, Kathy Whitacre, Paul Villinski, Tom Vaught, Terry Knickerbocker, Paul Haynes, Max Blagg, Anita Madeira, James Chambers, Gordon Minette, Bobby Ursino, Marla Kittler, Allen Coulter, Elaine Ramseyer, Ryan Maher, Neil, Andrew and Amanda Trout, Wendy, Ralphie and Becky St. John, Phillip, Emily, Matthew and Luke McQuillan, and mom and dad.

And love and affection to Duane Cerney for trying to make the most of it.

About the Author

Linda St. John's work has appeared in galleries and museums across the country. She has been a featured artist in *The New Yorker*, *Ms.*, *Art in America*, and *Time Out New York*. She is married to photographer Duane Cerney, and together with their daughter, Suzi Galloway, they own a gallery/store called D.L. Cerney in Manhattan. The art on the jacket is original work by Linda St. John.

A Note about the Type

The text of this book was set in Iowan Old Style. Iowan Old Style was designed for Bitstream in 1991 by noted sign painter John Downer. Iowan Old Style is a hardy contemporary text design that is classified as Venetian old style; it is modeled after earlier twentieth-century revivals of Jenson and Griffo typefaces but with a larger x-height, tighter letter fit, and reproportioned capitals. In designing Iowan, John Downer also took inspiration from classical inscriptional lettering and sign painting seen in certain regions of eastern Iowa.